# Disneyland Paris Travel Guide 2024

*Essential Tips and Hidden Gems for Budget-Friendly Family Adventures*

**Walter L. Wilkerson**

Copyright © 2024 **Walter L. Wilkerson**

All rights reserved.
No part of this publication may be produced, distributed, or transmitted in any form or by any means, including photocopying, recording, or other electronic or mechanical methods without the prior written permission of the publisher, except in the case of brief quotations embodied in critical reviews and certain other noncommercial uses permitted by copyright law.

Copytighted Material

## About The Author

Walter L. Wilkerson is a distinguished travel guide writer, adventurer, and publisher whose passion for exploration has taken him to the farthest corners of the globe. With a career spanning over two decades, Walter has crafted an impressive portfolio of travel guides that capture the essence of his journeys with a unique blend of detail and narrative flair. His work is characterized by a deep commitment to uncovering the hidden gems of each destination, offering readers an insider's perspective that goes beyond the typical tourist experience.

Born with an insatiable curiosity and a love for storytelling, Walter embarked on his first solo adventure in his early twenties, igniting a lifelong pursuit of travel. His expeditions have led him through bustling cities, serene countrysides, remote islands, and ancient landmarks, enriching his understanding of diverse cultures and histories. This extensive experience is reflected in his writing, where he combines meticulous research with personal anecdotes, bringing each location to life for his readers.

Walter's travel guides are celebrated for their comprehensive detail, practical advice, and engaging style, making them indispensable companions for travelers worldwide. As a publisher, he has also championed new voices in travel writing, fostering a community of adventurers and storytellers who share his dedication to exploration and cultural discovery.

Whether trekking through the Amazon rainforest or wandering the streets of Paris, Walter L. Wilkerson continues to inspire and guide travelers with his boundless enthusiasm and expert insights.

## About the Book

Dive into the enchantment of Disneyland Paris with the "Disney Paris Travel Guide 2024," your ultimate companion for experiencing the magic like never before. Crafted by renowned travel writer and adventurer Walter L. Wilkerson, this guide is more than just a book—it's your key to unlocking a world of wonder, thrills, and unforgettable memories.

Bursting with in-depth insights, the guide covers every corner of Disneyland Paris, from the nostalgic charm of Main Street, USA, to the adrenaline-fueled adventures of Frontierland. Discover the hidden treasures of Adventureland, the whimsical fantasies of Fantasyland, and the cinematic magic of Walt Disney Studios Park. Each page is packed with detailed descriptions, practical tips, and vibrant anecdotes, ensuring you're well-prepared for every moment of your visit.

This 2024 edition brings you the latest updates, including new attractions, seasonal events, and insider tips to make the most of your trip. Whether you're a first-time visitor or a seasoned Disney enthusiast, you'll find valuable information on everything from booking tickets and accommodations to dining with beloved Disney characters and navigating the parks with ease.

The "Disney Paris Travel Guide 2024" is designed to cater to all, whether you're planning a family vacation, a romantic getaway, or an adventurous solo trip. Walter L. Wilkerson's engaging style and expert knowledge provide a unique blend of comprehensive detail and captivating storytelling, making this guide an indispensable resource for your magical journey.

Prepare to be enchanted—Disneyland Paris awaits, and with this guide in hand, the magic is yours to explore!

## HOW TO USE THE QR CODE MAP

Upon scanning the QR code, you'll be automatically directed to your Google Maps app. Enter your current location and tap "Directions" to receive accurate guidance to your desired destination. This demonstrates the ease and convenience of using the QR code for detailed navigation information.

**Paris Charles de Gaulle Airport**
95700 Roissy-en-France, France
3.6 ★★★★★  60,832 reviews
View larger map

## Scan this QR Code

- Open your camera app: Launch the camera application on your smartphone.
- Point at the QR code: Aim your camera at the QR code, ensuring the code is centered and clear.
- Hold steady: Keep your phone steady and wait for a notification or prompt.
- Tap the notification: When a notification appears, tap it to open the link or content.
- Follow the instructions: Follow any additional prompts to complete the action (e.g., opening a website).

Copytighted Material

6

### Disneyland Park

**Disneyland Park**
Disneyland Paris, Bd de Parc, 77700 Chessy, France
4.6 ★★★★★ 33,890 reviews
View larger map

## Scan this QR Code

- **Open your camera app:** Launch the camera application on your smartphone.
- **Point at the QR code:** Aim your camera at the QR code, ensuring the code is centered and clear.
- **Hold steady:** Keep your phone steady and wait for a notification or prompt.
- **Tap the notification:** When a notification appears, tap it to open the link or content.
- **Follow the instructions:** Follow any additional prompts to complete the action (e.g., opening a website).

Copytighted Material

7

## Parc Walt Disney Studios

Pl. des Frères Lumière, 77700 Chessy, France

4.6 ★★★★★  75,310 reviews

View larger map

## Scan this QR Code

- Open your camera app: Launch the camera application on your smartphone.
- Point at the QR code: Aim your camera at the QR code, ensuring the code is centered and clear.
- Hold steady: Keep your phone steady and wait for a notification or prompt.
- Tap the notification: When a notification appears, tap it to open the link or content.
- Follow the instructions: Follow any additional prompts to complete the action (e.g., opening a website).

Copytighted Material

Walt Disney World

Parade Masquade

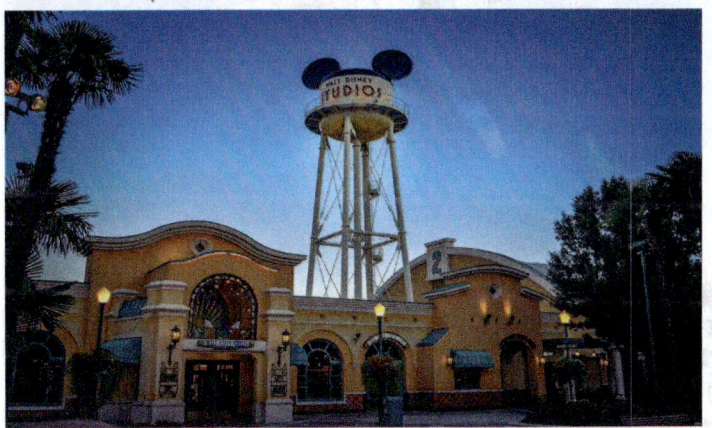

Disneyland, Disney.

# Table of Contents

| | |
|---|---|
| **About The Author** | **2** |
| **About the Book** | **4** |
| **Contents** | **11** |
| **Introduction** | **16** |
| **Chapter 1** | **18** |
| **Introducing Disneyland Paris** | **18** |
|    Welcome to Disneyland Paris | 19 |
|    Why Visit Disneyland Paris in 2024? | 19 |
|    Tip for First-Time Visitors | 22 |
| **Chapter 2** | **25** |
| **Plan Your Trip** | **25** |
|    Best Time to Visit | 26 |
|    How to Get There | 27 |
|    Hotel and Accommodation Options | 29 |
|    Booking Tickets | 31 |
|    Recommended Itinerary Ideas | 35 |
| **Chapter 3** | **38** |
| **Disneyland Park** | **38** |
|    Main Street, U.S.A. | 39 |
|    Frontierland | 41 |
|    Adventureland | 43 |
|    Fantasyland | 47 |
| **Chapter Walt Disney Studios Park** | **49** |
|    Front Lot | 50 |

Copytighted Material

| | |
|---|---|
| Production Courtyard | 51 |
| Toon Studio | 53 |
| Backlot | 55 |

**Chapter 5** — **57**
**Must-See Attractions** — **57**

| | |
|---|---|
| Dumbo, The Flying Elephant | 58 |
| Sleeping Beauty Castle | 58 |
| Pirates of The Caribbean | 59 |
| Skull Rock - A Musical Landmark | 59 |
| Big Thunder Mountain | 60 |
| Swiss Family Treehouse | 60 |
| Space Mountain: Mission 2 | 61 |
| Worlds of Pixar | 62 |
| Pirate's Beach | 63 |
| Adventurer's Playground | 63 |
| Phantom Manor | 64 |
| Peter Pan's Flight | 64 |
| Suspension Bridges | 64 |
| Alice's Curious Labyrinth | 65 |
| Buzz Lightyear Laser Blast | 65 |
| The Twilight Zone: Tower of Terror | 66 |
| Crush's Coaster | 66 |
| Snow White & the Seven Dwarfs | 67 |
| Toy Story: Playland | 67 |
| Studio Tram Tour: Behind the Magic | 67 |
| Mickey and the Magician | 68 |

**Chapter 6**   **70**
**Dining in Disneyland Paris**   **70**
   Prompt Service Restaurants   71
   Casual Dining   72
   Fine Dining   73
   Character Dining   74
   Special Dietary Options   75
   Snacks and Treats   76

**Chapter 7**   **78**
**Entertainment and Shows**   **78**
   Daily Parades   79
   Nighttime Showcases   79
   Seasonal Shows and Events   80
   Character Meet & Greets   81

**Chapter 8**   **84**
**Tips for Families - Creating Magical Memories with Your Kids at Disneyland Park**   **84**
   Top Attractions for Kids: Adventure Awaits!   85
   Stroller Rentals: Keep Up with Little Explorers   87
   Child-Friendly Dining: Preparing for Adventure   88
   Planning with Young Children: Making Lasting Memories   89

**Chapter 9**   **91**
**Igniting the Spark—A Guide to Romance at Disneyland Park**   **91**
   Romantic Park Spots: Tranquility and Togetherness

Copytighted Material

92
    Adult-Friendly Attractions: Excitement and Laughter for Two     93

    Romantic Dining: An Evening of Culinary Delights   94

    Nightlife Experiences: A Park Transformed     95

    Couples Photo Opportunities: Capturing Memories 96

**Chapter 10**     **98**

**Waltzing Through the Seasons—A Guide to Disneyland Park's Annual Events and Festivals**   **98**

    Overview of Annual Events     99

**Chapter 11**     **102**

**A World for Everyone—Accessibility and Special Needs at Disneyland Park**     **102**

    Services for Guests With Disabilities     103

    Accessible Attractions and Rides     104

    Dietary Accommodations     104

    Assistance Animals     105

    Special Passes and Privileges     106

**Chapter 12**     **108**

**Safe and Sound: A Guide to Safety and Security at Disneyland Park**     **108**

    Park Rules & Regulations     109

    Lost and Found     110

    Emergency Services     111

    Health and Safety Guidelines     111

**Chapter 13**     **113**

Copytighted Material

**Beyond the Magic Gates: Exploring Paris and the Environs**   **113**
- Jurassic Park at Disneyland    114
- Paris City Highlights: A City Rich in History and Beauty    115
- Château de Versailles: A glimpse into French opulence    118
- Vald'Europe Shopping Center: A Shopaholic's Paradise    121
- Aquatonic Spa    123

**Chapter 14**    **126**
**Frequently Asked Questions - Navigating Your Parisian Adventure Easily**    **126**
- Common Inquiries    127
- Tips from Experienced Visitors    128
- Troubleshooting and Problem-solving    129

**Chapter 15**    **131**
**Final Tips and Advice for Polishing Your Parisian Gem**    **131**
- Making the Most of Your Visit: Enjoy the Parisian Pace    132
- Insider Tips: Paris Secrets Revealed    133
- Packing List: Essentials for a Paris Adventure    134
- Departure Day Tips: Ensure a Smooth Takeoff    135

**Conclusion**    **137**
- Appendix    139
- Glossary for Disney Paris Travel Guide 2024    142

Copytighted Material

# Introduction

Welcome to the "Disney Paris Travel Guide 2024," your guide to the magic and wonder of Disneyland Paris. Imagine a land where fairy tales come to life, aspirations soar to new heights, and the mundane disappears into a realm of pure enchantment. This book is your indispensable companion, designed to help you navigate and thoroughly immerse yourself in the captivating pleasures that await you in the heart of France's most enchanted kingdom.

Disneyland Paris is more than simply a theme park; it's a breathtaking tapestry of narrative and adventure, expertly woven into the fabric of two enthralling parks: Disneyland Park and Walt Disney Studios Park. Each land in these parks is a portal to a distinct realm of fantasy, from the nostalgic streets of Main Street, USA to the exotic rainforests of Adventureland, the wild frontiers of Frontierland, and the fanciful joys of Fantasyland. Prepare to be captivated as you explore these fantasy settings, which are packed with classic attractions, magnificent performances, and popular Disney characters.

The following sections include a wealth of information that will help you make the most of your stay. Discover the ideal times to go to avoid crowds, the most convenient transportation options, and insider advice for making the most of your stay. Learn about the many ticket options, special discounts and packages, and numerous lodging alternatives, ranging from opulent Disney hotels to lovely neighboring inns.

Our guide goes beyond the essentials, delving into the enchantment with thorough explanations of must-see sights, eating experiences, and entertainment choices. Whether you want to experience the excitement of Space Mountain, the charm of It's a Small World, or the majesty of Disney Illuminations, we've got you covered. Special sections on seasonal events, character meet-and-greets, and VIP experiences can help you personalize your stay.

So collect your loved ones, pack your sense of wonder, and prepare to journey into a realm where magic exists and dreams come true. The journey of a lifetime awaits at Disneyland Paris, and with the "Disney Paris Travel Guide 2024" in hand, you'll be well prepared to enjoy it all. Let the magic begin!

# Chapter 1

## Introducing Disneyland Paris

Embark on a journey to the heart of magic and imagination with Disneyland Paris. In this chapter, we'll explore the enchanting world of Disneyland Paris, a destination where dreams come true and memories are made. Discover the rich history, fascinating attractions, and endless entertainment that await you in the most magical place on earth. Join us as we delve into the wonder and excitement of Disneyland Paris and prepare to experience the adventure of a lifetime.

## Welcome to Disneyland Paris

Disneyland Paris, located in the lovely town of Marne-la-Vallée, about 48 kilometers (29.8 miles) east of Paris, is a magnificent destination that attracts millions of people each year. This popular resort, which opened on April 12, 1992, has developed to become one of Europe's top family attractions. Disneyland Paris' precise coordinates are 48.8674°N latitude and 2.7833°E longitude. As you enter this beautiful realm, you'll be surrounded by a blend of old Disney charm and innovations that are sure to fascinate guests of all ages.

Disneyland Paris is more than simply a theme park; it's a place where fairy tales come true, where the thrill of adventure meets the delight of discovery, and where the enchantment of Disney storytelling can be found around every corner. From meeting your favorite characters to seeing world-class attractions, Disneyland Paris provides a one-of-a-kind entertainment experience that promises to create memories that will last a lifetime.

## Why Visit Disneyland Paris in 2024?

2024 is building up to be an incredible year for Disneyland Paris, with various new experiences and upgrades aimed to excite guests. Here are some convincing reasons to make 2024 the year you visit this magnificent place:

1. Disneyland Paris' 30th-anniversary festivities, which began in 2022, will continue until 2024 with spectacular events, parades, and performances honoring the resort's rich past and promising future. Expect special events, limited-edition goods, and holiday décor to lend an additional layer of magic to your experience.

2. New Attractions: Disneyland Paris is always growing, with new attractions and experiences set to open in 2024. Keep a watch out for new additions to Disneyland Park and Walt Disney Studios Park, which promise to provide new thrills and adventures.

3. Seasonal Events: Disneyland Paris is famous for its seasonal festivals. Whether it's the eerie fun of Halloween, the charming celebrations of Christmas, or the brilliant allure of spring and summer events, there's always something unique going on. These events will be even more stunning in 2024, with new shows, décor, and character encounters.

4. Technological enhancements: The resort is investing in new technology to improve the visitor experience. These updates, which range from app-based services that make it easier to organize your day to advancements in vehicle technology, guarantee that your stay runs smoothly and enjoyable.

5. Sustainability measures: Disneyland Paris is devoted to sustainability and has launched several measures to lessen its environmental effects. From energy-efficient structures to waste-reduction measures, the resort is working toward a greener future. Visiting in 2024 allows you to enjoy the wonder while also supporting a commitment to environmental responsibility.

6. Gastronomic Delights: Disneyland Paris' eating scene is always evolving, with new restaurants and menus offering a wide variety of gastronomic pleasures. From gourmet meals to simple snacks, there's something for everyone's taste. Look forward to eating new cuisines and revisiting old favorites in wonderfully designed settings.

7. Ease of Access: With changes to transportation infrastructure, traveling to Disneyland Paris is now

simpler than ever. Whether you arrive by aircraft, rail, or automobile, the resort is well-connected and accessible, making it an ideal location for both foreign and local visitors.

## Tip for First-Time Visitors

Planning your first trip to Disneyland Paris might be daunting, but with a few pointers, you can make the most of your wonderful vacation.

1. Plan your visit during the shoulder seasons—spring (March to May) and fall (September to November). During these times, the weather is good, and the crowds are lower than during peak summer months and holidays.

2. Accommodation: Staying at one of Disney's on-site hotels has various benefits, including Extra Magic Time, which allows you to visit the parks before they open to the general public. Popular choices include the Disneyland Hotel (48.8730° N latitude, 2.7799° E longitude), which provides elegant lodgings and convenient access to the park gates, and Disney's Sequoia Lodge (48.8690° N latitude, 2.7877° E

Copytighted Material

longitude), which is recognized for its rustic appeal and proximity to Disney Village.

3. Ticket Options: Buy your tickets in advance to avoid long lineups at the gate and take advantage of special deals. If you want to spend many days exploring both parks, consider purchasing a multi-day pass. The Disneyland Paris app is an excellent resource for managing your tickets and organizing your vacation.

4. Arrive before the parks open to make the most of your day. This is especially crucial if you wish to visit famous sights that have reduced wait periods. If you're staying at a Disney hotel, take advantage of Extra Magic Time to get an early start on the day.

5. Navigation: Get acquainted with the park maps and the Disneyland Paris app. The app gives you real-time updates on wait times, show schedules, eating alternatives, and more. Use it to efficiently traverse the parks and maximize your time.

6. Prioritize Attractions: Create a list of must-see attractions and performances and base your itinerary around them. Prioritize popular rides such as Big

Thunder Mountain, Ratatouille: The Adventure, and the Twilight Zone Tower of Terror to avoid large lines later in the day.

7. Dining Reservations: Make reservations in advance, particularly for table-service restaurants. Popular restaurants like Bistrot Chez Rémy (48.8674° N latitude, 2.7740° E longitude) and Auberge de Cendrillon (48.8712° N latitude, 2.7768° E longitude) fill up quickly, so reserve your space to enjoy a stress-free lunch.

8. Comfy Footwear: Disneyland Paris requires a lot of walking, so wear comfy shoes. It's also a good idea to dress in layers because the weather changes throughout the day.

9. Remind Hydrated and Take Breaks: Pack a refillable water bottle to remain hydrated. Take frequent stops to relax and recharge, especially if you are visiting with young children. Designated rest places and shaded locations around the parks offer a break from the congestion and bustle.

10. Record the Memories: Remember to bring your camera or smartphone to record those beautiful

moments. Take advantage of PhotoPass services to get professional images with characters and at renowned locations.

Visiting Disneyland Paris is an adventure into a world of magic and excitement. With careful planning and these helpful hints, your first visit will be full of delight, amazement, and great experiences.

# Chapter 2

# Plan Your Trip

Planning your trip to Disneyland Paris is an exciting adventure in itself, filled with anticipation and excitement for the magical experiences that await you. In this chapter, we'll guide you through the essential steps of planning your visit, from choosing the best time to travel to selecting accommodation options and booking tickets. Whether you're a first-time visitor or a seasoned Disney enthusiast, careful planning ensures that your trip is as seamless and enjoyable as possible. Join us as we embark on the journey of planning your dream vacation to the happiest place on earth.

## Best Time to Visit

Timing your visit to Disneyland Paris may significantly improve your experience, allowing you to avoid crowds and inclement weather. Disneyland Paris is best visited during the shoulder seasons, which are spring (March to May) and fall (September to November). During these times, the weather is often pleasant, and the parks are less crowded than during peak summer months and big holidays.

Springtime in Disneyland Paris is beautiful, with blooming flowers and temperatures ranging from 10°C (50°F) to 20°C (68°F). Events like the Spring Festival feature spectacular parades and floral displays, making it a wonderful time to visit.

Fall provides stunning fall landscapes and milder weather, with temperatures ranging from 10°C (50°F) to 18°C (64°F). Halloween festivities begin in late September, with frightening décor, themed events, and special character meet-and-greets.

Avoid Peak Times: To have a more relaxing stay, avoid school vacations, big holidays such as Christmas and New Year's, and the summer months of July and August.

During certain seasons, the parks are usually more crowded, and wait times for attractions might be much longer.

## How to Get There

Disneyland Paris is easily accessible from many regions of Europe and beyond. Here's the easiest method to get there:

### By Plane

The nearest airport to Disneyland Paris is Charles de Gaulle Airport (CDG), which is around 40 kilometers (24.8 miles) away. CDG's coordinates are 49.0097° North latitude and 2.5479° East longitude. From the airport, take the TGV (high-speed rail) to Marne-la-Vallée/Chessy station, which is only a two-minute walk from the park's gates. The trip takes around 10 minutes.

Alternatively, Orly Airport (ORY), located 47 kilometers (29.2 miles) from Disneyland Paris, is another possibility. The coordinates are 48.7284° N latitude and 2.3794° E longitude. From Orly, use the Magical Shuttle bus service, which runs every day and takes around 60 minutes to reach the resort.

**By Train**

Disneyland Paris is well-connected by train, making it a great location for visitors from all across Europe. The Marne-la-Vallée/Chessy station (48.8704° N latitude and 2.7807° E longitude) is located just adjacent to the park gates and acts as a significant hub for many rail services.

The TGV (High-Speed Train) connects Disneyland Paris with major French cities and other European locations. For example, the ride from Paris Gare de Lyon to Marne-la-Vallée/Chessy takes only 35 minutes.

**Eurostar:** If you're coming from the UK, Eurostar offers direct service from London St Pancras International to Marne-la-Vallée/Chessy. The trek takes around 2 hours and 45 minutes.

**RER (Regional Train):** The RER A line links downtown Paris to Disneyland Paris. The trip from Châtelet-Les Halles station takes around 40 minutes.

**By Car**

Driving to Disneyland Paris is simple, as the resort is well-signposted from the main roads. The address for GPS navigation is Boulevard de Parc, 77700 Coupvray,

France. Its coordinates are 48.8708°N latitude and 2.7831°E longitude.

From Paris, take the A4 (Autoroute de l'Est) and follow the signs to Disneyland Paris. The trip takes around 40 minutes, depending on traffic. The resort offers parking, including allocated spots for Disney hotel guests.

## Hotel and Accommodation Options

Disneyland Paris has a variety of lodging alternatives to suit different tastes and budgets. Here are some of the better options.

### Disneyland Hotels

Staying at a Disney hotel offers a variety of advantages, including early park entry, complimentary shuttle services, and immersive theming.

1. Disneyland Hotel: This Victorian-style hotel, located at the entrance to Disneyland Park, provides magnificent rooms and outstanding service. The coordinates are 48.8730° North latitude and 2.7799° East longitude.

2. Disney's Newport Bay Club is a nautical-themed hotel inspired by New England's coastal resorts. It's a

15-minute walk from the parks, at 48.8702° N latitude and 2.7896° E longitude.

3. Disney's Sequoia Lodge: Nestled among beautiful foliage, this rustic lodge provides a warm, cabin-like environment. It's a 10-minute walk from the parks, located at 48.8690° N latitude and 2.7877° E longitude.

4. Disney's Hotel Cheyenne: This Wild West-themed hotel exudes Old West charm. The coordinates are 48.8695° N latitude and 2.7985° E longitude; the parks are a 20-minute walk or a brief shuttle ride away.

**Partner Hotels**
Partner hotels are located near Disneyland Paris and provide a blend of comfort and cost. They often offer shuttle service to the parks.

1. Vienna House Magic Circus: This circus-themed hotel is ideal for families and features a variety of services. It is situated at 48.8685° North latitude and 2.7920° East longitude.

2. B&B Hotel: A low-cost choice with modern conveniences, the B&B Hotel is a 10-minute shuttle ride

from the parks. The coordinates are 48.8700°N latitude and 2.8057°E longitude.

**Nearby Hotels**
For those who prefer to remain offsite, various hotels in the surrounding region provide easy access to Disneyland Paris.

1. Radisson Blu Hotel Paris, Marne-la-Vallée: This upmarket hotel features golf course views and a variety of services. It is situated at 48.8595° North latitude and 2.8070° East longitude.

2. Hotel l'Elysée Val d'Europe: Located in the Val d'Europe retail center, this hotel provides convenient access to shopping and eating alternatives. The coordinates are 48.8553°N latitude and 2.7712°E longitude.

## Booking Tickets

When planning your trip, reserving tickets ahead of time may save you both time and money. Here are some important considerations:

**Types of Tickets**

Disneyland Paris provides a variety of ticket choices to meet different needs:

1. One-Day Tickets: These tickets are ideal for short visits because they grant entrance to one or both parks for a single day. Prices vary according to the season and park access.

2. Multi-Day Tickets: For a more complete experience, multi-day tickets provide entrance to both parks on numerous days. These tickets are a better bargain than purchasing single-day tickets for each day of your vacation.

3. Annual passes provide unrestricted entry to the parks as well as extra benefits such as savings on eating, shopping, and hotel stays.

**Special Offers and Packages**

Keep an eye out for unique deals and packages that will improve your Disneyland Paris experience.

1. Seasonal Promotions: Disneyland Paris frequently provides discounts and special packages at specific

periods of the year. These promos might include lower ticket costs, complimentary food plans, or reduced hotel rates.

2. Package Deals: Booking a vacation package that includes park tickets, lodging, and meals can result in big discounts. These packages sometimes feature extra benefits like early park admission and character dining experiences.

Budgeting for Your Trip
Planning a vacation to Disneyland Paris requires careful budgeting to ensure that you get the most out of your experience without overpaying.

**Estimated Costs**
Here's a general breakdown of the average expenditures for a family of four visiting Disneyland Paris for three days:

1. Accommodation: Depending on the accommodation, expect to pay between €300 and €1,200 each night. Staying at a Disney hotel often costs extra but provides additional perks.

2. Park Tickets: Depending on the season and ticket type, multi-day tickets for two people and two children can range from €600 to €1,000 for a three-day visit.

3. Dining: Expect to spend between €50 and €100 per person each day on meals, snacks, and drinks. Dining at table-service restaurants will be more costly than quick-service establishments.

4. Consider transportation expenditures such as airline, train tickets, or gasoline for driving. Hotel packages typically include shuttle service and public transportation inside the resort.

5. Souvenirs & Extras: Plan for additional costs such as souvenirs, pictures, and unique experiences such as character eating. A realistic estimate is €50-€100 per person.

**Money Saving Tips**
Here are some ways to save money on your Disneyland Paris trip:

1. Book ahead of time to take advantage of early bird discounts and special deals on tickets and accommodations.

2. Travel During Off-Peak Seasons: Visiting during the shoulder seasons results in not only fewer crowds but also reduced rates for accommodations and tickets.

3. Bring Your Snacks: To save money on meals, bring your snacks and drinks. There are several designated picnic sites across the parks.

4. Consider staying at a partner hotel, which frequently provides affordable prices and shuttle service to the parks.

5. Use the Disneyland Paris App: The app offers real-time information on wait times and food alternatives, allowing you to organize your day more effectively and save unnecessary spending.

6. Take Advantage of Free Activities: Free entertainment options include parades, performances, and character meet-and-greets, which add to the magic at no additional expense.

By preparing ahead of time and making wise decisions, you can have a fantastic Disneyland Paris visit that suits your budget and leaves lasting memories for your family.

## Recommended Itinerary Ideas

Calling all families, thrill-seeking youngsters, and lovebirds in search of Parisian enchantment! Disneyland Paris isn't just a park, it's a portal to endless possibilities. But with two parks, dazzling shows, and captivating characters, where do you even begin? Fear not, fellow adventurers, for this guide unveils a treasure trove of itinerary ideas, tailored to unleash the magic for every kind of traveler!

### For the Fun-Sized Adventurers:

*Day 1:* Embark on a whirlwind adventure through Fantasyland, meeting classic Disney characters and soaring on iconic rides like Peter Pan's Flight. Explore Adventureland, where pirates plunder and Indiana Jones seeks lost treasures. End the day with a dazzling fireworks display, leaving little eyes wide with wonder!

*Day 2:* Channel your inner space ranger in Walt Disney Studios! Blast off on thrilling Star Wars: Hyperspace Mountain, and assemble with your favorite Marvel heroes in the all-new Avengers Campus. Little ones will adore the whimsical world of Cars and the playful antics of Toy Story characters.

***Day 3:*** Take a break from the park frenzy! Relax at your Disney hotel pool, indulge in a character breakfast, or explore the charming Disney Village with its bustling shops and delectable restaurants. A character meet-and-greet here might just be the cherry on top of a magical trip!

**For the Young Thrill-Seekers:**

***Day 1:*** Conquer the heart-pounding heights of Big Thunder Mountain Railroad in Frontierland. Challenge the gravity-defying loops of Space Mountain: Mission 2 in Discoveryland. In the afternoon, cool off with a thrilling splash on Pirates of the Caribbean.

***Day 2:*** Test your bravery in Walt Disney Studios! Face the hair-raising descent of The Twilight Zone Tower of Terror™, and scream your way through the Hollywood Tower Hotel. Later, channel your inner rockstar on the heart-stopping Rock 'n' Roller Coaster Starring Aerosmith.

***Day 3:*** Take a detour to explore the spooky secrets of Phantom Manor in Disneyland Park. Enjoy a thrilling stunt show in Walt Disney Studios, and unleash your competitive spirit on the classic RC Racer attraction.

**For the Lovebirds Seeking Parisian Magic:**

*Day 1:* Start your romantic adventure with a character breakfast, followed by a leisurely stroll down Main Street, U.S.A. Indulge in a candlelit dinner at one of the park's exquisite restaurants, serenaded by the park's enchanting music. Cap off the night with a front-row seat for the dazzling fireworks display.

*Day 2:* Embark on a romantic boat ride through the fantastical world of "It's a Small World." Share a laugh on the playful Pirates of the Caribbean boat ride, and lose yourselves in the captivating beauty of the nighttime illuminations.

*Day 3:* Venture beyond the park gates and explore the charming city of Paris. Stroll hand-in-hand along the Seine, marvel at the Eiffel Tower, and soak up the city's romantic atmosphere. Return to the park for a final magical evening, savoring the park's captivating ambiance.

Remember, these are just starting points! With this guide as your compass, customize your itinerary to create an unforgettable Disney Paris adventure, just for you!

# Chapter 3

# Disneyland Park

Welcome to the Happiest Place on Earth: Detailed Tour of Disneyland Park

Ah, Disneyland Park! The very term conjures up visions of happy youngsters, exciting rides, and Mickey Mouse himself. Since its grand inauguration in 1955, this legendary park in Anaheim, California (33°80′24″N 117°49′12″W) has been inspiring dreams and creating memories. Today, we'll go on a wonderful tour around its most cherished lands, taking in the sights, sounds, and tales that have made Disneyland a truly worldwide phenomenon.

## Main Street, U.S.A.

Main Street U.S.A.

Main Street, U.S.A. is your entry point to Disneyland Park, recreating the charm and nostalgia of a turn-of-the-century American village. With coordinates of 48.8717° N latitude and 2.7796° E longitude, this region greets you with its scenic streets, horse-drawn streetcars, and bustling atmosphere.

As you go along Main Street, U.S.A., you'll see a variety of businesses and restaurants. The Emporium, a huge store with a great selection of Disney items, is a must-visit. For a lovely eating experience, visit the Plaza Gardens Restaurant, which offers a buffet in a Victorian-era setting.

The Main Street Vehicles are one of the most popular attractions on Main Street, USA. These historic vehicles and horse-drawn streetcars offer a unique way to go up and down the street, taking you on a leisurely tour of this attractive neighborhood. Don't miss the Dapper Dans, a live barbershop quartet that will bring an element of nostalgia to your stay.

Throughout the day, Main Street, U.S.A. morphs into a venue for numerous parades and performances.

Disney Stars on Parade is a daily event in which famous characters are brought to life in a colorful procession with extravagant floats and fascinating music. The nightly show, Disney Illuminations, takes place at Sleeping Beauty Castle, which can be seen from Main Street. It blends explosions, projections, and music for a spectacular end to your day.

Main Street, USA also provides a variety of

Services to help you enjoy your stay. The City Hall, located near the entrance, provides guest relations services such as bookings and park information. The Main Street Fire Station is nearby and provides a nice photo opportunity as well as a testimony to Walt Disney's commitment to preserving heritage.

## Frontierland

Frontierland, located at 48.8710° N latitude and 2.7774° E longitude, immerses visitors in the harsh character of the American Old West. This place is a monument to pioneers and explorers, with thrilling rides and attractions that capture the spirit of the frontier.

Big Thunder Mountain is a signature attraction at Frontierland. This runaway mine train roller coaster will take you through the twists and turns of an abandoned mining town. The ride is both thrilling and visually gorgeous, with a rich landscape that enhances the experience.

Phantom Manor is another must-see attraction. This spooky haunted home provides a spine-tingling journey through a mansion full of ghosts and monsters. The attraction's intricate plot and superb visual effects make it a popular choice among thrill seekers.

The Rivers of the Far West provide a more relaxing experience. You may enjoy a leisurely boat trip on the

Mark Twain Riverboat or the Molly Brown, both of which provide gorgeous views of Frontierland's scenery. The riverboats offer a unique view of the park, allowing you to appreciate the nuances and beauty of the surroundings.

Frontierland also has several food alternatives. The Lucky Nugget Saloon offers Western-themed meals with live entertainment. The Cowboy Cookout Barbecue is ideal for individuals who want to enjoy a substantial supper in a rural atmosphere.

Frontierland features seasonal events and shows all year long, adding to the excitement in the neighborhood. During Halloween, the area is transformed with eerie decorations and themed activities, bringing another dimension of enjoyment to your sta

## Adventureland

Adventureland, Disneyland Park.

Adventureland, at 48.8727° N latitude and 2.7757° E longitude, is a land of discovery and excitement. This region is inspired by exotic settings and adventure stories, with attractions that transport you to faraway lands.

Pirates of the Caribbean is one of Adventureland's primary attractions. This famous boat ride takes you through scenarios from pirate life, including animatronic pirates, riches, and sea warfare. The intricate settings and engaging storyline make it a timeless classic.

For adrenaline fans, Indiana Jones and the Temple of Peril is a must-see. This roller coaster, based on a well-known archeologist, takes you through an ancient temple at top speeds. The attraction's steep dips and abrupt turns give an adrenaline rush for those seeking adventure.

Adventure Isle is another attraction of this location. This interactive area includes caverns, suspension bridges, and hidden treasures that are ideal for adventurers of all ages. The Swiss Family Treehouse, inspired by the Disney film, provides panoramic vistas from its high vantage point as well as insight into the Robinson family's existence.

Dining options at Adventureland are as diverse as the activities. Captain Jack's - Restaurant des Pirates provides an unforgettable dining experience within the Pirates of the Caribbean rollercoaster. The cuisine includes seafood and Creole-inspired dishes, creating a gourmet excursion that complements the surroundings.

Throughout Adventureland, you will find stores selling exotic items and themed stuff. La Girafe Curieuse and Les Trésors de Schéhérazade are excellent places to buy mementos and one-of-a-kind goods to remember your stay.

**Fantasyland:** Fantasyland is the center of Disneyland Park's magic, where fairy stories come to life. This dynamic location, situated at 48.8738° N latitude and 2.7750° E longitude, is home to several renowned attractions and amazing experiences.

The Sleeping Beauty Castle is the showpiece of Fantasyland. This landmark monument, with its towering spires and elegant architecture, is a must-see. Inside the castle, you may see La Galerie de la Belle au Bois Dormant, which portrays the story of Sleeping Beauty via exquisite stained glass windows and tapestries.

Peter Pan's Flight is one of the most popular attractions in Fantasyland. This nighttime trip transports you above London and into Neverland, following Peter Pan and the Darling children. The ride's breathtaking scenery and smooth flying route make it a favorite among tourists of all ages.

It's a Small World is another popular attraction in Fantasyland. This boat excursion has dolls from all around the world performing the popular song "It's a

Small World." The vibrant displays and catchy melody make for a fun experience that honors worldwide unity and diversity.

Alice's Curious Labyrinth provides a distinct type of experience. This labyrinth, inspired by Alice in Wonderland, allows you to explore the story's characters and situations as you meander through the hedges. The Queen of Hearts Castle, located in the middle, provides an excellent perspective over Fantasyland.

Dining choices in Fantasyland include Auberge de Cendrillon, which allows you to dine in a storybook setting with Cinderella and her entourage. The restaurant serves French cuisine and has a wonderful environment, making for a great lunch.

Shops in Fantasyland, such as La Chaumière des Sept Nains and La Boutique du Château, sell Disney-themed products. These businesses are ideal for purchasing souvenirs and presents to commemorate your stay.

## Discoveryland

Discoveryland, Disneyland Park.

Discoveryland, located at 48.8720° North latitude and 2.7756° East longitude, is a land of futuristic adventure and ingenuity. This section is inspired by the ideas of famous thinkers and innovators, and it has attractions that explore the wonders of science and imagination.

Space Mountain: Mission 2 is one of Discoveryland's highlights. This roller coaster transports you to the depths of space, providing high-speed thrills and breathtaking views. The attraction's unique concept and thrilling ride experience make it a must-see for adrenaline junkies.

Buzz Lightyear Laser Blast is another popular activity at Discoveryland. This interactive attraction allows you to join Buzz Lightyear in his struggle against the villainous Emperor Zurg. With a laser blaster, you may fire targets and compete for the greatest score, making it an enjoyable and engaging experience for people of all ages. The Nautilus offers a more relaxing experience. This walkthrough experience, based on Jules Verne's "20,000 Leagues Under the Sea," takes visitors into Captain Nemo's submarine. The realistic settings and interactive features create an immersive experience in the world of undersea exploration. Café Hyperion, located at Discoveryland, serves a range of fast food options in a futuristic environment. The restaurant's vast dining space and entertainment make it an ideal spot to relax and recharge. Discoveryland also has stores like Constellations and Star Traders, where you can buy a range of space-themed items and souvenirs. These businesses sell a variety of things, including toys, clothing, collectibles, and gifts. Discoveryland provides spectacular events and shows throughout the year, adding to the excitement in the region.

# Chapter 4

# Walt Disney Studios Park

Walt Disney Studios Park, located at 48.8683° N latitude and 2.7819° E longitude, is an intriguing part of Disneyland Paris. This park is dedicated to the worlds of movies, television, and entertainment, allowing visitors to experience the magic behind the screen. This chapter digs into the park's four major areas: front lot, production courtyard, toon studio, and backlot. Each sector contains distinct attractions, culinary options, and experiences that bring the world of cinema to life.

# Front Lot

The Front Lot at Walt Disney Studios Park greets guests with the glamor and enchantment of Hollywood's Golden Age. It acts as a doorway to the remainder of the park, establishing the tone for the upcoming cinematic experiences.

Upon approaching the Front Lot, visitors are greeted by the magnificent Disney Studio 1 edifice. This remarkable edifice, located at 48.8675° N latitude and 2.7815° E longitude, has a variety of stores and restaurants. The inside is supposed to look like a Hollywood film set, replete with neon lights, movie posters, and classic facades. It provides an insight into the sparkle and glamour of old Hollywood.

The Walt Disney Studios Store is one of Disney Studio 1's key attractions. This store sells a large variety of Disney items, including garments, toys, and souvenirs. It's the ideal spot to pick up a souvenir from your trip or locate gifts for friends and family at home.

Front Lot has a variety of restaurants that appeal to different preferences. Restaurant en Coulisse is a popular option, serving quick cuisine in a setting that resembles a backstage studio canteen. The décor and setting take diners to the middle of a bustling movie studio, giving an unforgettable dining experience.

The Front Lot also features various meet-and-greet areas where customers may connect with their favorite Disney characters. Whether it's Mickey Mouse, Minnie Mouse, or another famous figure, these encounters give spectacular photo opportunities and lasting memories.

Furthermore, the Front Lot serves as the primary location for park services. Guest Relations, located near the entrance, may assist with tickets, bookings, and general concerns. This section also offers stroller rentals, locker rentals, and first aid, ensuring that guests have all they need for a relaxing and pleasurable day at the park.

## Production Courtyard

The Courtyard, located at 48.8672° N latitude and 2.7822° E longitude, is the hub of the filmmaking process at Walt Disney Studios Park. This section immerses viewers in the behind-the-scenes world of film creation, with activities that demonstrate the magic of filmmaking. The Twilight Zone Tower of Terror is one of the most impressive attractions in the Production

Courtyard. This exhilarating ride leads passengers on a terrifying adventure through a haunted hotel, culminating in a sequence of shocking drops. The attraction's intricate theming and dramatic atmosphere make it a must-see for thrill lovers.

Cinemagique, another famous attraction, combines live performance with cinema. This performance takes audiences on a trip through cinema history, incorporating classic sequences from well-known films. The seamless mixing of live performers with on-screen action results in an immersive and enjoyable experience.

The Studio Tram Tour: Behind the Magic also takes place in the Production Courtyard. This guided tour provides tourists with a behind-the-scenes peek at several film sets and special effects. The tour includes a visit to Catastrophe Canyon, where tourists may see a spectacular exhibition of realistic effects utilized in action movies.

For eating, Production Courtyard has alternatives such as the Blockbuster Café. This restaurant serves a meal inspired by popular movies and has themed dining spaces that commemorate various film genres. It's an excellent spot to take a rest and dine while immersed in the cinematic ambiance.

In addition to activities and food, Production Courtyard features a variety of live acts and events throughout the year. These performances allow audiences to experience the enchantment of entertainment up close, as skilled actors, dancers, and musicians bring stories to life.

## Toon Studio

Toon Studio, located at 48.8667° North latitude and 2.7808° East longitude, brings the world of animated films to life. This lively section highlights animation talent, with attractions and experiences based on popular Disney and Pixar characters.

Ratatouille: The Adventure is one of Toon Studio's highlights. This 4D dark experience transports guests through the streets of Paris via the eyes of Remy, the charming rodent from Disney-Pixar's "Ratatouille." This attraction is a tourist favorite because of its revolutionary ride technology, rich scenery, and immersive storytelling experience. Crush's Coaster is another famous attraction at Toon Studio. This spinning roller coaster sends riders on an undersea voyage with Crush, the laid-back sea turtle from "Finding Nemo." The coaster boasts exhilarating drops and turns, making it a fun and exciting experience for customers of all ages.

Cars Quatre Roues Rallye provides a fun ride for the whole family. Inspired by the "Cars" movies, this attraction allows visitors to take a spin in multicolored cars that twist and whirl around the track. It's a fantastic trip that reflects Radiator Springs' charm and excitement.

Toon Studio also has character meet-and-greet areas where visitors may engage with their favorite cartoon characters. From Woody and Buzz Lightyear to Elsa and Anna, these meetings give spectacular moments and photo possibilities that will be remembered for years.

Toon Studio's dining offerings include Bistrot Chez Rémy, a themed restaurant that immerses customers in the world of "Ratatouille." The restaurant's décor makes visitors feel as if they've been downsized to the size of a rat, with huge furnishings and adorable accents that bring the film to life. The menu offers French cuisine, which provides a wonderful and engaging eating experience.

Toon Studio also has various stores that sell a range of items. These stores provide anything from toys and clothes to memorabilia and artwork, making it easy to bring a bit of the enchantment home with you.

## Backlot

Backlot, located at 48.8661° N latitude and 2.7814° E longitude, is Walt Disney Studios Park's most action-packed region. This area concentrates on the high-energy world of action films, with attractions and experiences including spectacular stunts and amazing effects.

Backlot's major attraction is the Moteurs... Action! Stunt Show Spectacular. This live performance comprises experienced stunt artists who conduct high-speed automobile chases, motorbike leaps, and pyrotechnic effects. The show gives viewers an exhilarating behind-the-scenes peek at how action sequences are made for the big screen.

Another popular attraction on Backlot is the Rock 'n' Roller Coaster, which stars Aerosmith. This indoor roller coaster takes passengers on a high-speed journey through a sequence of twists and turns to the music of

Aerosmith. The attraction's blend of exhilarating ride features and rock-and-roll music makes it a hit with adrenaline addicts.

Armageddon - Les Effets speciaux is an interactive experience that explains how special effects are used in movies. Guests may see a meteor impact recreated with fire, smoke, and explosions, offering an intriguing glimpse at the craft of practical effects.

Backlot's dining choices include Café des Cascadeurs, a retro-style diner serving a range of American cuisine. The restaurant's classic décor and casual ambiance make it an ideal location to unwind and eat.

Backlot also has stores where people may purchase movie-related products. These stores provide anything from garments and accessories to souvenirs and memorabilia that celebrate cinema's enchantment.

Backlot organizes special events and performances all year long, adding to the area's energy. These events frequently include unique entertainment, interactive activities, and themed décor that contribute to the overall mood of Walt Disney Studios Park.

# Chapter 5

# Must-See Attractions

Disneyland Paris has a variety of attractions that guarantee to delight people of all ages. Each ride and show is precisely crafted to provide exceptional experiences, combining immersive narrative with cutting-edge technology. In this chapter, we'll look at some of the must-see sights, explaining what makes each one distinctive and why you should include them on your schedule.

## Dumbo, The Flying Elephant

Dumbo the Flying Elephant is a famous amusement that both children and adults enjoy. Located in Fantasyland (coordinates: 48.8735° N latitude, 2.7760° E longitude), this amusing attraction lets tourists fly through the air on the back of Dumbo, the famed flying elephant. Riders have control over the height of their elephant, offering a sensation of freedom and adventure. The colorful ride vehicles and upbeat music make it a fun experience for families

## Sleeping Beauty Castle

Sleeping Beauty Castle

The Sleeping Beauty Castle, also known as "Le Château de la Belle au Bois Dormant," is Disneyland Park's renowned centerpiece. The castle, located at 48.8738° N latitude and 2.7750° E longitude, rises magnificently at the end of Main Street in the United States of America. Its spectacular design, inspired by

French fairy tales and actual castles, has soaring turrets, stained glass windows, and detailed decorations. Inside, guests may explore La Galerie de la Belle au Bois Dormant, a stunning exhibition that depicts Sleeping Beauty's narrative via tapestries, sculptures, and artwork. La Tanière du Dragon, an animatronic dragon that breathes smoke and movements, is located beneath the castle, adding to the mystery and thrill.

## Pirates of The Caribbean

Pirates of the Caribbean is an exciting boat ride that takes passengers through a succession of scenarios featuring swashbuckling pirates and their adventures. This attraction, located in Adventureland (coordinates 48.8727° N latitude, 2.7757° E longitude), is well-known for its immersive surroundings and sophisticated animatronics. The journey starts in a peaceful Caribbean bay and takes you through pirate-infested waterways, a pirate ship combat, and a besieged settlement. The cheerful theme tune, "Yo Ho (A Pirate's Life for Me)," contributes to the attraction's charm and popularity.

## Skull Rock - A Musical Landmark

The renowned Skull Rock, a colossal skull-shaped rock structure that serves as more than a visual background, towers over Adventureland's entrance. Keep your ears open, since this rock is home to a chorus of singing pirates! Throughout the day, disembodied pirate voices emerge from the skull, entertaining park visitors with sea shanties and pirate anthems. It's a unique and surprising touch that enhances Adventureland's immersive feel.

## Big Thunder Mountain

Big Thunder Mountain is a thrilling mining train roller coaster located in the harsh terrain of Frontierland. This attraction's coordinates are 48.8710° North latitude and 2.7774° East longitude. The attraction, known for its high-speed twists and turns, transports guests on a thrilling excursion through an abandoned mining town packed with tunnels, caves, and deadly drops. The intricate theming and spectacular effects, like dynamite blasts and waterfalls, heighten the sense of adventure and excitement.

## Swiss Family Treehouse

The Swiss Family Robinson Treehouse, a renowned symbol since Disneyland's opening day, provides more than simply breathtaking vistas. Climb the creaky wooden steps that spiral around the enormous edifice, and you'll be transported to the world of the famous novel. Explore the different rooms, which are beautifully crafted to replicate the Robinsons' ramshackle house. Peer out the windows for stunning views of the park, or simply admire the brilliance and workmanship that went into designing this classic attraction.

These are just a handful of the hidden gems to be uncovered throughout Disneyland Park. So, the next time you come, take a break from the big attractions and go on a mission to discover these hidden jewels. You might be shocked by the wonder you discover!

## Space Mountain: Mission 2

Space Mountain: Mission 2, located in Discoveryland (coordinates: 48.8730° N latitude, 2.7769° E longitude), is an indoor roller coaster that transports visitors on an exciting voyage through space. The journey includes high-speed twists, turns, and inversions, all against a backdrop of stars and cosmic occurrences. The mix of darkness, fantastic effects, and powerful music results in a thrilling experience that should not be missed.

## Worlds of Pixar

Entrance of Pixar Amusement Park

Prepare to shrink down to toy size and discover the colorful world of Toy Story Playland, Walt Disney Studios Park's newest attraction. This place brings the renowned Pixar film to life, with giant structures that resemble classic toys such as Slinky Dog and Woody. Enjoy a thrilling trip on Slinky Dog Dash, a high-speed coaster that runs through Andy's backyard. For a more relaxing experience, ride the spinning Toy Soldiers

Parachute Drop and take in the beautiful views of the park from above.

## Pirate's Beach

Pirate's Beach is tucked away in the corner of Adventureland, providing a sanctuary for young scallywags. This sandy play area is a pirate's dream come true, complete with a shipwreck to explore, rigging to climb, and water cannons to fire (be prepared to get soaked!). Parents may rest on adjacent seats while their children channel their inner Captain Hook by looking for hidden riches and creating their swashbuckling adventures.

## Adventurer's Playground

Adventureland's dense greenery conceals a hidden gem: Explorer's Playground. This interactive play area is intended to inspire children's spirit of exploration. Kids may crawl over rope bridges, negotiate secret corridors, and climb across decrepit bridges, all while feeling as if they've discovered a lost realm. Keep an eye out for the naughty chimps that live in this region; they are known for bringing a dash of unexpected excitement (and maybe a sprinkle of trouble) to the tour.

## Phantom Manor

Phantom Manor is a haunted house attraction located in Frontierland (48.8712° N latitude, 2.7775° E longitude). This spooky ride follows the story of a bride who was abandoned at the altar and now haunts the mansion with ghostly apparitions. Guests are taken through dark and eerie sceneries complete with elaborate animatronics, special effects, and a chilling soundtrack. Phantom Manor's intricate storyline and evocative architecture make it a must-see for enthusiasts of ghost stories and the uncanny.

## Peter Pan's Flight

Peter Pan's Flight is a popular nighttime ride in Fantasyland (coordinates: 48.8732° N latitude, 2.7762° E longitude). This captivating spectacle transports visitors across London and into Neverland aboard a flying pirate ship. The ride incorporates sequences from the original Disney film, such as meetings with Peter Pan, Wendy, Captain Hook, and the Lost Boys. The mix of vivid sights and a sense of flying makes this ride a favorite among tourists of all ages.

## Suspension Bridges

For those looking for adventure without the adrenaline rush of a large ride, the park has various suspension bridges that give a unique view. In Adventureland, locate the bridge that connects the Swiss Family Robinson Treehouse to the mainland. As you wobble on the undulating wooden planks, you'll get a bird's-eye view of the lush forest below and the busy crowds traversing the park. Similarly, in Frontierland, Tom Sawyer Island has a suspension bridge with breathtaking vistas of the Rivers of America and the Mark Twain Riverboat chugging along.

## Alice's Curious Labyrinth

Alice's Curious Labyrinth is an interactive walk-through maze in Fantasyland (48.8740° N latitude, 2.7752° E longitude). Inspired by Disney's "Alice in Wonderland," this attraction takes visitors on a journey through meandering walkways, fascinating gardens, and enchanting landscapes starring narrative characters. The aim is to reach the Queen of Hearts' Castle, which provides a panoramic perspective of the park. The whimsical style and fascinating puzzles make this an enjoyable experience for families.

## Buzz Lightyear Laser Blast

Buzz Lightyear Laser Blast, located in Discoveryland (coordinates: 48.8728° N latitude, 2.7771° E longitude), is an interactive shooting ride in which guests assist Buzz Lightyear destroy the villainous Emperor Zurg. Riders use laser blasters to shoot at targets throughout the ride, earning points and competing against one another. The brilliant colors, loud music, and friendly rivalry make this a really exciting attraction.

## The Twilight Zone: Tower of Terror

The Twilight Zone Tower of Terror, located at Walt Disney Studios Park's Production Courtyard (48.8660° N latitude, 2.7794° E longitude), is a terrifying drop tower ride set in an ominous, abandoned hotel. Inspired by the legendary television series "The Twilight Zone," the attraction has a complex plot and outstanding special effects. Guests endure a series of dives and rises, generating a sensation of weightlessness and suspense that is both thrilling and scary.

## Crush's Coaster

Crush's Coaster, located in Toon Studio (coordinates: 48.8669° N latitude, 2.7805° E longitude), is a spinning roller coaster that takes guests on an underwater adventure with Crush, the sea turtle from Disney-Pixar's "Finding Nemo." The ride combines dark ride elements with coaster thrills, with scenes of the Great Barrier Reef, jellyfish fields, and the East Australian Current. This attraction stands out for its spinning ride vehicles and vibrant sights.

## Snow White & the Seven Dwarfs

Snow White and the Seven Dwarfs is a popular dark ride located in Fantasyland (48.8736° N latitude, 2.7759° E longitude). This attraction portrays the story of Snow White through a succession of brilliantly constructed scenarios using animatronics and vivid settings. Guests go through the Evil Queen's palace, the magical woodland, and the dwarfs' home before ending at Snow White's happily ever after. The ride's timeless appeal and intricate narration make it a favorite among Disney enthusiasts.

## Toy Story: Playland

Toy Story Playland, located in Walt Disney Studios Park's Toon Studio (coordinates: 48.8672° N latitude, 2.7811° E longitude), is an immersive area based on the popular "Toy Story" movie. The area has various attractions, including "RC Racer," a thrilling half-pipe ride, "Toy Soldiers Parachute Drop," a family-friendly free-fall ride, and "Slinky Dog Zigzag Spin," a pleasant spinning ride for smaller children. The big toys and bright colors create a fun and engaging atmosphere.

## Studio Tram Tour: Behind the Magic

The Studio Tram Tour: Behind the Magic, located in Walt Disney Studios Park's Backlot (coordinates: 48.8652° N latitude, 2.7832° E longitude), provides guests with a behind-the-scenes glimpse at the filmmaking process. The tour takes tourists through several movie sets, including the "Catastrophe Canyon" special effects area, where they may witness an earthquake, fire, and water firsthand. The educational discussion and live demonstrations offer insights into the filming process.

## Mickey and the Magician

Mickey Mouse, Disneyland.

Mickey and the Magician is a stunning stage play at Walt Disney Studios Park's Animagique Theater (48.8675° N latitude, 2.7798° E longitude). The performance stars Mickey Mouse as an aspiring magician who learns magic secrets from other Disney characters such as Genie, Elsa, and Rafiki. The presentation mixes breathtaking special effects, precise choreography, and famous Disney melodies to create a unique and unforgettable experience.

Disneyland Paris has a diverse range of attractions that cater to every taste and age group. From the fanciful appeal of Fantasyland to the thrilling adventures of Adventureland and the cinematic wonders of Walt Disney Studios Park, each attraction is designed to give a distinct and immersive experience. Disneyland Paris delivers unlimited wonder and adventure, whether you're flying over Neverland with Peter Pan, exploring the spooky hallways of Phantom Manor, or assisting Buzz Lightyear in defeating Emperor Zurg.

# Chapter 6

# Dining in Disneyland Paris

Disneyland Paris is more than just thrilling rides and fascinating shows; it's also a gastronomic destination with a diverse range of dining options. Whether you want a fast snack, a casual dinner, or a gourmet dining experience, you'll find something to suit your taste. In this chapter, we will look at the many eating options offered at Disneyland Paris, so you know where to go for the best meals during your vacation.

## Prompt Service Restaurants

Quick-service restaurants are ideal for visitors who wish to eat while still enjoying the park's attractions. These eateries serve a variety of foods, from burgers and fries to healthier options such as salads and wraps.

### Hyperion Cafe

Hamburger

Hyperion Cafe, located in Discoveryland (48.8723° N latitude, 2.7770° E longitude), is Disneyland Park's largest quick-service restaurant. It serves American-style fast cuisine such as hamburgers, chicken nuggets, and salads. The huge dining space is fashioned after a big theater and frequently has live entertainment on stage, creating a vibrant and immersive dining experience.

### Casey's Corner

Casey's Corner, located on Main Street in the United States (coordinates: 48.8718° N latitude, 2.7795° E longitude), is a must-see for hot dog lovers. This baseball-themed restaurant serves a range of gourmet hot dogs, chips, and refreshing drinks. The retro design and outdoor seats make it an ideal place to unwind and admire the scenery of Main Street.

### Hakuna Matata Restaurant

Hakuna Matata Restaurant is located in Adventureland (coordinates: 48.8725° N latitude, 2.7756° E longitude) and was inspired by Disney's "The Lion King." The menu includes African-inspired foods including kebabs, rice, and salads. The vivid, themed design and delectable food make it an excellent dining choice for families.

### Casual Dining

For a more comfortable eating experience with table service, Disneyland Paris' casual dining options offer a variety of cuisines and atmospheres.

### Bistro Chez Rémy

Bistro Chez Rémy, located at Walt Disney Studios Park's Toon Studio (coordinates: 48.8676° N latitude, 2.7804° E longitude), provides a unique dining experience inspired by the Disney-Pixar film "Ratatouille." The restaurant reduces people to the size of rats, complete with gigantic furnishings including huge dishes and utensils. The menu includes French cuisine, such as ratatouille, sirloin, and a range of great wines.

### Captain Jack's – Restaurant des Pirates

Captain Jack's - Restaurant des Pirates, located in Adventureland (coordinates 48.8728° N latitude, 2.7754° E longitude), offers a

75

Caribbean eating experience just inside the Pirates of the Caribbean attraction. The darkly lit tropical environment is complemented by the sound of water and pirate-themed décor. The menu has seafood, pork dishes, and vegetarian alternatives, making it ideal for a sit-down supper.

**Plaza Garden Restaurant**

Plaza Gardens Restaurant, located on Main Street, USA (coordinates: 48.8721° N latitude, 2.7793° E longitude), provides a beautiful Victorian setting with a buffet-style eating experience. Salads, pasta, meats, and desserts are among the many foreign foods served at the restaurant. Its pleasant environment and wide food make it a popular choice among families.

**Fine Dining**

Disneyland Paris has a variety of exquisite dining alternatives that are sure to satisfy your palate.

**Cendrillon Auberge**

Auberge de Cendrillon, located in Fantasyland (48.8737° N latitude, 2.7752° E longitude), is a fairy-tale-themed restaurant where customers can eat with Disney Princesses. The sophisticated French cuisine includes gourmet meals including foie gras, roasted meats, and delectable desserts. The lovely atmosphere and character interactions make for an unforgettable eating experience.

Inventions, located in the Disneyland Hotel (coordinates: 48.8719° N latitude, 2.7792° E longitude), serves a lavish buffet with a view of Disneyland Park. The menu offers a diverse selection of foreign meals, with a focus on seafood and excellent meats. Guests may enjoy their dinner in the elegant settings while seeing Disney characters, which adds a magical touch to their dining experience.

### California Grill

California Grill, located at the Disneyland Hotel (48.8720° N latitude, 2.7791° E longitude), serves a refined menu of French and Californian fusion cuisine. The restaurant's exquisite design and panoramic views of the park provide an ideal backdrop for a memorable supper. Fresh seafood, excellent steaks, and an extensive wine list are some of the highlights.

### Character Dining

Character eating is a must-do experience that mixes delicious cuisine with Disney enchantment. These restaurants provide an opportunity to meet popular Disney characters while having a tasty dinner.

### Cendrillon Auberge

As previously stated, Auberge de Cendrillon in Fantasyland offers a delightful dining experience featuring Disney Princesses. The exquisite atmosphere and gourmet meal, mixed with character encounters, make it ideal for families and admirers of the Disney monarchy.

**Plaza Garden Restaurant**

Plaza Gardens Restaurant on Main Street, U.S.A. serves character breakfasts in addition to buffets. Guests may begin their day with a substantial lunch and meet Mickey Mouse, Minnie Mouse, and other beloved characters. The mix of good cuisine and memorable events makes it an ideal way to start the day at the park.

**Cafe Mickey**

Café Mickey, located in Disney Village (48.8685° N latitude, 2.7804° E longitude), is a bustling restaurant where tourists may dine with famous Disney characters. The menu has a mix of Italian and American foods, including pizzas, pasta, and burgers. The entertaining atmosphere and character appearances make it popular with both youngsters and adults.

**Special Dietary Options**

Disneyland Paris is devoted to serving customers with particular dietary requirements. Many restaurants cater to persons with food allergies, intolerances, or dietary restrictions.

**Allergies and intolerances**

Most restaurants at Disneyland Paris can accommodate customers with dietary allergies and intolerances. It is suggested that you notify the restaurant staff of any dietary needs when making a reservation or upon arrival. Many restaurants include gluten-free, lactose-free, and nut-free alternatives to ensure that all visitors enjoy their meals safely.

**Vegetarian and Vegan Options**
Vegetarian and vegan meals are offered at a variety of food establishments across the park. Plant-based cuisine is available at restaurants such as Hyperion Cafe and Captain Jack's - Restaurant des Pirates, providing vegetarians and vegans with tasty options. Furthermore, Disney's dedication to providing varied and inclusive eating options ensures that new vegetarian and vegan meals are launched regularly.

**Halal and Kosher Meals**
Halal and kosher meals can be reserved in advance at some eateries. Guests are recommended to contact Disneyland Paris' guest services or dining reservations staff to discuss their dietary requirements and guarantee that appropriate meals are provided.

**Snacks and Treats**
In between attractions and performances, Disneyland Paris provides a selection of refreshments and delicacies to keep you refreshed and satisfied.

## Popcorn with Churros

**Churros**

Popcorn and churros are popular delicacies sold at carts and stalls throughout the park. The sweet and salty tastes make them ideal for snacking on the road.

## Ice cream with Pastries

For those with a sweet craving, there are several ice cream and pastry selections. The Gibson Girl Ice Cream Parlour (coordinates: 48.8718° N latitude, 2.7794° E longitude) on Main Street, U.S.A., offers a variety of ice cream flavors, while the Cable Car Bake Shop serves wonderful pastries and baked goods.

## Mickey-shaped Treats

No trip to Disneyland Paris is complete without indulging in Mickey-shaped delicacies. From cookies and waffles to pretzels and ice cream bars, these popular snacks are both delicious and photogenic.

Dining at Disneyland Paris is a gastronomic journey that adds to the enchanting experience of the parks. Whether you want a fast nibble, a leisurely lunch, or fine dining, there's something for everyone's taste and choice. The broad selection of eating options, along with the captivating theming and character encounters, guarantees that each meal is a highlight of your stay. As you visit the parks, take time to sample the delectable culinary and dining experiences that Disneyland Paris has to offer.

# Chapter 7

# Entertainment and Shows

Entertainment is central to the Disneyland Paris experience, with a dazzling selection of parades, evening spectaculars, seasonal events, and character meet-and-greets to enchant guests of all ages. In this chapter, we'll look at the resort's numerous entertainment options, making sure you don't miss out on any of the excitement throughout your vacation.

## Daily Parades

Disney Stars on Parade

Disney Stars on Parade is a colorful parade that brings famous Disney characters to life through song, dancing, and spectacle. This parade, which features carefully crafted floats, bright costumes, and vivacious performers, celebrates the wonder of Disney stories. Guests may join Mickey Mouse, Minnie Mouse, and their pals as they go across Disneyland Park, waving and dancing to delightful songs.

## Nighttime Showcases

Disney Illuminations is a stunning nightly show that transforms Sleeping Beauty Castle into a magnificent canvas of light, color, and sound. This multimedia spectacular blends cutting-edge projections, fireworks, and special effects to bring legendary Disney stories to life in a breathtaking visual spectacle. From classic stories like "The Lion King" and "Frozen" to current favorites like "Star Wars" and "Moana," Disney Illuminations transports visitors on an extraordinary trip through the realm of Disney enchantment.

## Seasonal Shows and Events

### Halloween

During the Halloween season, Disneyland Paris transforms into a spooky wonderland complete with festive decorations, themed rides, and unique entertainment offers. Guests may participate in Halloween-themed events, parades, and character meet & greets, as well as immersive activities such as haunted mazes and trick-or-treat trails. From scary meetings with Disney villains to joyful festivities with Mickey and his pals, Halloween at Disneyland Paris is a frightfully delightful event for the entire family.

Disneyland Paris celebrates Christmas with festive decorations, lighting, and seasonal entertainment, creating a magnificent atmosphere. Guests may experience spectacular Christmas parades, stunning light displays, and heartfelt stage presentations starring their favorite Disney characters. Special events, such as Mickey's Magical Christmas Lights and Disney's Christmas Parade, add to the holiday atmosphere, while festive snacks and goods make it simple to get into the season.

**New Year's Eve**

Disneyland Paris' New Year's Eve event is unlike any other, with thrilling entertainment, breathtaking fireworks, and a celebratory environment. Guests may celebrate the new year with live concerts, dance celebrations, and unique dining experiences at the parks and Disney Village. As the clock strikes midnight, fireworks illuminate the sky above Sleeping Beauty Castle, providing a magnificent background for the start of the new year.

## Character Meet & Greets

Meeting Disney characters is a highlight of each trip to Disneyland Paris, allowing visitors to meet with their favorite heroes, heroines, and villains in person. Throughout the parks, you'll have countless opportunities to meet legendary Disney characters, take photographs, and get signatures, resulting in cherished experiences that will last a lifetime. Everyone may enjoy traditional characters like Mickey Mouse and Cinderella, as well as modern favorites like Elsa and Spider-Man.

**Character Locations**

Character meet and greet sites may be located around Disneyland Paris, allowing visitors to meet their favorite characters in a variety of themed settings. Whether it's seeing Mickey Mouse on Main Street, U.S.A., participating in a princess parade in Fantasyland, or discovering superheroes at Walt Disney Studios Park, there's always a spectacular moment to be discovered.

**Photo Opportunities**

Photo opportunities with Disney characters are offered at designated meet-and-greet spots, where customers may pose for photos and create memories with their favorite characters. Disney PhotoPass photographers are available to snap professional-quality images, ensuring that every memory is cherished for years to come. Guests may also use their cameras and cellphones to snap photographs with the characters, resulting in unique souvenirs of their stay.

**Autograph and Interactions**

In addition to posing for pictures, Disney characters like interacting with customers by signing autographs, hugging, and participating in lighthearted chats. Whether it's exchanging a high-five with Buzz Lightyear, receiving a royal handshake from a princess, or dancing with Winnie the Pooh, interactions with Disney characters are guaranteed to make people of all ages smile.

## Special Experiences
### Dining With Characters
Dining with Characters allows customers to eat a wonderful meal while interacting with renowned Disney characters in a unique and immersive environment. Disneyland Paris offers a variety of eating options, including character breakfast buffets and themed dinners, where guests may meet Mickey Mouse, Minnie Mouse, and their pals up close. These experiences allow guests to spend magical moments with their favorite characters while eating delicious food, making it a memorable addition to any trip to the resort.

### VIP Tours
VIP Tours provide tourists with the ultimate Disneyland Paris experience, with exclusive access to attractions, entertainment, and eating options. These trips are conducted by professional guides and offer bespoke itineraries tailored to each group's interests and preferences. Whether you want to bypass the lines, see your favorite characters, or enjoy a private fireworks show, a VIP Tour guarantees a spectacular day at the

park. VIP Tours provide guests the luxury of preferential access and intimate information, resulting in remarkable encounters that transcend expectations.

Entertainment and events are an essential element of the Disneyland Paris experience, allowing visitors to immerse themselves in the enchantment of Disney narrative. Everyone will find something to enjoy, from daily parades and nightly spectaculars to seasonal events and character meet-and-greets.

## Chapter 8

## Tips for Families - Creating Magical Memories with Your Kids at Disneyland Park

Disneyland Park is a delight for kids of all ages. From the exhilarating plunges of Splash Mountain to the colorful wonderland of Fantasyland, the park provides limitless opportunities to create great experiences. However, navigating a theme park with small children may be a thrilling experience in and of itself. Fear not, tired parents! This chapter will help you arrange a pleasant and exciting visit to Disneyland Park with your children.

## Top Attractions for Kids: Adventure Awaits!

Disneyland Park caters excellently to children, with a wealth of rides and attractions designed to pique their interest and fire their sense of wonder. Here's a summary of some surefire hits for each age group:

### For Toddlers (Under 3 years old):
Fantasyland attractions include It's a Small World (a pleasant boat ride symbolizing world unity), Winnie the Pooh (a honey-filled excursion through the Hundred Acre Wood), and Storybook Land Canal Boats.

Mickey's Toontown has Mickey and Minnie's residences (meet-and-greets with beloved characters) and Gadget's Go Coaster (a mild spinning coaster ideal for first-time visitors).

Main Street, USA: Disneyland Railroad (a picturesque train trip around the park) and Main Street Electrical Parade (a nightly extravaganza of glittering lights and music).

### For Preschoolers (ages 3–5):
Fantasyland attractions include Peter Pan's Flight, Mr. Toad's Wild Ride, and King Arthur Carrousel.

Adventureland includes the Jungle Cruise (a funny boat excursion with cheeky monkeys and tumbling waterfalls) and The Enchanted Tiki Room (a Polynesian-themed performance with singing animatronic birds).

Frontierland attractions include the Big Thunder Mountain Railroad (a runaway mining train experience) and the Mark Twain Riverboat (a picturesque paddle steamer trip throughout America's rivers).

**For School-Aged Children (Ages 6 and Up)**
Adventureland includes Indiana Jones Adventure (an exciting ride through booby-trapped temples) and Pirates of the Caribbean.

Tomorrowland: Buzz Lightyear Laser Blast (an interactive quest in which you may help Buzz beat Zurg), and Autopia (a traditional driving experience in future automobiles).

Fantasyland attractions include Matterhorn Bobsleds (a thrilling bobsleigh ride across the Matterhorn mountain) and "It's a Small World" (a timeless boat ride honoring worldwide harmony).

Remember, this is only the beginning point! With careful preparation and a little patience, you can customize your schedule to your children's individual interests and age groups. Don't be afraid to ask friendly cast members for ideas; they are professionals at creating memorable experiences for families.

## Stroller Rentals: Keep Up with Little Explorers

Those who do not want to carry their stroller can rent one at Disneyland Park. Single and double strollers are provided, making it easier to explore the park with young children in tow. Stroller rentals are available at the following locations:

**Main Entrance Stroller Rental:** Located on the left side of the Main Entrance, near the security screening area.

Fantasyland Stroller Rental: Located near the Fantasyland entrance and the "it's a small world" attraction.

**Pro-Tip:** Consider hiring a stroller for the full day, especially if you have little children who may tire quickly. Stroller rentals are available throughout the park and may be quite useful during lengthy days of exploring.

**Additional options:**

Locker rentals: Lockers are strategically positioned throughout the park to store bulkier things such as diaper bags and backpacks. This allows you to move freely throughout the park without being burdened down by stuff.

Rider Switch Service: This service allows parents with small children who do not match the height requirements for various rides to take turns enjoying the attraction. One parent waits with the child while the other travels, and they simply trade places. This guarantees that everyone may experience the thrills without having to wait too long.

## Child-Friendly Dining: Preparing for Adventure

A full stomach makes for a happy adventurer! Disneyland Park has a variety of food options to suit even the pickiest diners. Here are some kid-friendly options:

**Quick-Service Restaurants:** These establishments provide a casual eating experience with typical dishes such as burgers, fries, chicken tenders, and pizza. Popular alternatives include Plaza Inn (Main Street, U.S.A.), known for its exquisite Mickey Mouse-shaped cookies.

Cosmic Cantina (Tomorrowland) serves cosmic food with a space-age ambiance.

Royal Blue Bayou (Frontierland) - A one-of-a-kind dining experience within the Pirates of the Caribbean rollercoaster that serves up New Orleans-inspired food.

**Sit-Down Restaurants:** These provide a more formal eating experience, with table service and a larger menu selection. Family-friendly options include Blue Bayou Restaurant (Frontierland), an upmarket counterpart of the Royal Blue Bayou that serves great Californian cuisine.

Plaza Inn (Main Street, United States of America) - In addition to quick-service alternatives, they provide table-service eating in a wonderful Victorian environment.

Carnation Cafe (Main Street, USA) serves typical American comfort cuisine in a historic environment.

Pro-Tip: Many restaurants provide separate children's menus with smaller amounts and familiar meals. To avoid waiting in line, consider mobile ordering with the Disneyland app. Furthermore, some restaurants provide character dining experiences in which you may meet and greet popular Disney characters while eating your meal.

## Planning with Young Children: Making Lasting Memories

Planning a trip to Disneyland Park with young children needs some extra planning and preparation. Here are some suggestions to guarantee a seamless and beautiful event for everybody involved:

**Set Realistic Expectations:** Disneyland Park may be daunting for small children. Plan shorter days with plenty of time for naps and leisure.

**Arrive Early:** Arrive early at the park's opening to avoid congestion. This allows you to enjoy some of the most popular rides with less wait time.

**Utilize Rider Switch:** Take use of the Rider Switch service so that both parents may experience thrilling rides without having to wait twice.

**Download the Disneyland app:** This useful tool lets you check wait times, mobile order meals, find amenities like bathrooms and Baby Care Centers, and even hunt down your favorite Disney characters for meet-and-greet chances.

**Pack Smartly:** Bring sunscreen, hats, suitable walking shoes, a change of clothes in case of an accident, and a reusable water bottle to remain hydrated.

# Chapter 9

## Igniting the Spark—A Guide to Romance at Disneyland Park

Disneyland Park is not limited to families with little children. It's a wonderland for couples looking for a little whimsy, adventure, and renewed passion. Whether you're celebrating a special event or simply having a date night, the park has a plethora of attractions to help you make unforgettable memories together.

## Romantic Park Spots: Tranquility and Togetherness

As the crowds decrease, Disneyland Park transforms into a compelling setting for romance. Here are some beautiful spots to steal a kiss, have a passionate talk, or simply soak up the lovely atmosphere:

At sunset, take a picturesque cruise on the Mark Twain Riverboat around the Rivers of America (33°48′22″N 117°49′12″W). The smooth swaying of the boat, the soothing sounds of the river, and the spectacular vistas of the park at dusk create an extremely romantic atmosphere.

Disneyland's Sleeping Beauty's Castle, located at 33°48′22″N 117°49′13″W, transforms into a brilliant display at night. The castle is illuminated with hundreds of glittering lights, giving it a beautiful and unearthly aura. Stroll hand in hand around the surrounding Fantasyland, admiring the shining castle and fanciful ambiance.

Discover the French Quarter Courtyard at New Orleans Square (33°48′23″N 117°49′11″W), a hidden treasure away from the park. This lovely courtyard, complete with blooming flower beds and wrought-iron balconies, takes you to the heart of New Orleans. Mint Julep Bar serves beignets (fried pastries) as live jazz music plays in the background.

Pro-Tip: Disneyland has evening spectaculars such as "Disneyland Forever" (a beautiful fireworks show with iconic Disney music) and "Main Street Electrical Parade" (a vivid parade of lighted floats). While these gatherings might be busy, they provide a spectacular and communal experience to cap off a romantic evening.

## Adult-Friendly Attractions: Excitement and Laughter for Two

Disneyland Park is not only about princesses and pirates. It provides an exciting selection of attractions that are sure to get your pulse pounding and your laughter bursting. Here are a few ideas to spark some friendly rivalry and mutual enthusiasm:

**Guardians of the Galaxy - Mission:** Breakout! (Tomorrowland): Join Rocket and Groot from the Guardians of the Galaxy for an exciting escape adventure. This unique attraction features a free-fall aspect and an interactive queue, making it ideal for daring couples.

**Indiana Jones Adventure (Adventureland):** Prepare for a bumpy trip through booby-trapped temples and dangerous encounters with snakes and rolling rocks. This iconic attraction provides a balanced combination of thrills and excitement, making it ideal for couples looking for a shared adrenaline experience.

**Star Wars: Rise of the Resistance (Galaxy's Edge):** Join the Star Wars™ narrative and escape a First Order Star Destroyer. This immersive experience utilizes cutting-edge technology and visual effects, leaving you breathless and invigorated.

Pro tip: If you don't mind being separated for a brief amount of time, use Disneyland's Single Rider Line. This line may greatly minimize wait times, allowing you to enjoy more attractions together.

## Romantic Dining: An Evening of Culinary Delights

A beautiful evening demands a delicious lunch. Disneyland Park has an outstanding selection of eateries, ranging from informal cafés to fine dining venues. Here are a few ideas to tease your taste senses and set the tone for an unforgettable evening:

Blue Bayou Restaurant at Frontierland (33°48′23″N 117°49′10″W) offers a New Orleans-inspired dining experience. You'll be surrounded by a stunning nocturnal bayou setting while savoring delicious Cajun and Creole food.

Carthay Circle Restaurant, located at 33°48′22″N 117°48′59″W, transports visitors to Hollywood's Golden Age. Valid Disneyland Park entry is required for admittance. This beautiful restaurant has gorgeous Art decor and a menu of unique Californian cuisine. Enjoy a pre-fixe meal or à la carte cuisine made with the freshest seasonal ingredients.

Located at 33°48′22″N 117°49′14″W, Storybook Treats (Fantasyland) offers a delectable delicacy with a dash of whimsy and sweetness. This lovely bakery serves a wonderful range of homemade delicacies, such as the renowned Mickey Mouse-shaped churros and Sleeping Beauty's sparkling pink rose apple.

Pro-Tip: Make dinner reservations in advance, especially for famous places like Blue Bayou Restaurant. This eliminates the need to wait for a table, enabling you to fully enjoy your romantic evening.

## Nightlife Experiences: A Park Transformed

Disneyland Park undergoes a beautiful makeover after dark. The shimmering lights, stunning entertainment, and dynamic environment provide an ideal setting for a memorable evening. Here are some activities to incorporate into your romance itinerary:

**Disneyland Forever Fireworks:** As the night sky darkens, expect to be enchanted by the breathtaking "Disneyland Forever" fireworks show. This stunning performance includes brilliant pyrotechnics, mesmerizing projections on Sleeping Beauty's Castle, and unforgettable Disney music.

The popular Main Street Electrical Parade takes you on a fanciful twilight tour along Main Street, U.S.A. This iconic nocturnal extravaganza includes floats decked with thousands of dazzling lights, figures covered in pixie dust, and vibrant music that will have you humming along.

World of Color (Disney California Adventure Park - accessible via Disneyland Park with proper park admission): Experience a stunning evening show on the sparkling waters of Paradise Bay at Disney California Adventure Park. "World of Color" uses cutting-edge water effects, brilliant lighting, and a Disney tale to create a visually and audibly fascinating experience.

Pro tip: For nocturnal entertainment, arrive early to obtain a good viewing area. Consider using Disney Genie+ (a program that allows guests to schedule time slots for select attractions, including some evening spectaculars) to avoid huge lines at these popular events.

## Couples Photo Opportunities: Capturing Memories

Disneyland Park provides a plethora of wonderful backgrounds for creating amazing moments with your loved one. Here are a few ideas to inspire your creativity:

**In Front of Sleeping Beauty's Castle:** No trip to Disneyland is complete without taking a classic photo in front of the renowned Sleeping Beauty's Castle. Capture the wonder of the park with this classic fairytale background.

**Disneyland Railroad Train:** Take a picturesque ride on the Disneyland Railroad and grab a quirky shot as the train chugs down the rails. The lovely trains and old atmosphere create a picture-perfect scene.

**New Orleans Square at Night:** After dark, step into the center of New Orleans Square to capture the beautiful mood of its wrought-iron balconies, overflowing flower beds, and dazzling French Quarter lights.

Pro tip: Disneyland Park photographers are stationed throughout the park and may take professional-quality images of you and your significant other. These photographs are an excellent way to remember your big day.

Remember that a romantic Disneyland Park journey is about making lasting memories together. Accept the charm, share laughter and thrills, and let the park light the flame of love. With careful preparation and following suggestions, you can turn your Disneyland Park visit into a memorable romantic getaway.

Copytighted Material

# Chapter 10

# Waltzing Through the Seasons—A Guide to Disneyland Park's Annual Events and Festivals

H ello! Disneyland Park is more than simply a location for timeless entertainment; it also celebrates the changing seasons via vivid festivals, dazzling décor, and unique events. Throughout the year, the park alters to reflect the spirit of the season, providing unique experiences for visitors of all ages. This chapter will walk you through the thrilling world of Disneyland Park's annual offers.

## Overview of Annual Events

Disneyland Park has a diversified calendar of yearly events, each providing something unique. Here's a short look at what you can expect throughout the year:

**January - February:** Begin the year with the Lunar New Year festival, a lively celebration of Asian cultures including traditional performances, wonderful cuisine, and one-of-a-kind products.

**March - April:** Take part in the California excursion Food & Wine Festival, a fascinating culinary excursion that includes gourmet morsels from famous California chefs, cooking demos, and specialty drinks.

**Spring - Summer:** The park changes into a springtime wonderland, complete with blossoming flowers, Easter egg hunts, and special character visits. Later in the summer, be ready for hot fun with special water play zones and character encounters.

**Halloween Time (September - October):** Prepare for a frightfully exciting Halloween season! The park changes with eerie décor, trick-or-treating chances, and the exciting Oogie Boogie Bash, a separately ticketed

Halloween celebration at Disney California Adventure Park.

**Holidays at Disneyland Resort (November - December):** Experience the enchantment of the season with sparkling decorations, heartfelt entertainment, special character welcomes, and the renowned "A Christmas Fantasy" parade.

Pro-Tip: Special events frequently have particular dates and may require additional ticket sales. To avoid disappointment, visit the Disneyland Park website regularly for the most recent event details, and be sure to acquire the right tickets ahead of time.

**Highlights from each season**

Each season at Disneyland Park has its special charm. Let's go further at some of the highlights:

**Winter:** The Lunar New Year celebration adds a bright splash of color to the first months of the year. Stroll through artistically adorned places like Disney California Adventure Park's Lunar New Year Marketplace, see exciting dragon dances, and taste delicious Asian-inspired snacks.

**Springtime** brings a magical energy to the park. Enjoy the amusing Eggstravaganza hunt, in which youngsters may look for bright Disney character eggs all across the park. Witness the lively Disney Floral & Garden Festival at Disney California Adventure Park (usually held in the spring months), which features magnificent floral displays, interactive exhibits, and delectable springtime delicacies.

**Summer:** Beat the heat with splashtastic activities throughout the summer months. Cool off with thrilling water coasters like Splash Mountain and Grizzly River Run, or play in fun water play zones like Mickey's Toontown Toon-Up. Evenings come alive with the stunning "Main Street Electrical Parade," a nightly show featuring lighting floats and popular Disney characters.

Fall: Halloween transforms Disneyland Park into a hauntingly wonderful paradise. Experience the eerie thrills of the Haunted Mansion Holiday, a seasonal spin on the iconic Haunted Mansion attraction. Children may go trick-or-treating around the park, collecting delicious sweets from friendly characters. For an extra dose of Halloween excitement, try visiting the separately ticketed Oogie Boogie Bash at Disney California Adventure Park, which includes scary entertainment, trick-or-treating pathways, and unique character interactions.

Winter vacations are a very lovely time at Disneyland Park. Immerse yourself in the holiday atmosphere with stunning decorations, lovely snowfall on Main Street, U.S.A., and the renowned "A Christmas Fantasy" procession with Santa Claus and his reindeer. Enjoy holiday-themed food and beautiful live performances that celebrate the enchantment of Christmas.

## Chapter 11

# A World for Everyone—Accessibility and Special Needs at Disneyland Park

Disneyland Park seeks to provide a spectacular and inclusive experience for all. The park provides a variety of services, resources, and accommodations to ensure that people with disabilities can enjoy everything it has to offer. This chapter will help you navigate Disneyland Park with specific requirements.

## Services for Guests With Disabilities

Disneyland Park recognizes that each guest has distinct demands. The following are some of the services offered to guarantee a smooth and comfortable visit:

**Disability Access Service (DAS):** This free service allows guests with impairments who may struggle to wait in typical lines to register for a return time for specific attractions.

Guest Relations rents out assistive listening devices, which augment sounds for guests with hearing problems.

Visual cues: Many attractions use visual cues (such as flashing lights) to accompany aural statements.

**Handheld Captioned Phones:** Guests with hearing problems can speak with Cast Members (Disneyland Park staff).

**Wheelchair Rentals:** Wheelchairs are available at the Main Entrance Stroller Rental location. Electric Conveyance Vehicles (ECVs) are also available for rental, depending on availability.

Pro-Tip: Before you come, download the Disneyland Park app. The app lets you see accessibility information for rides and attractions, find accessible facilities and eateries, and check wait times with DAS return window availability.

## Accessible Attractions and Rides

Disneyland Park has a wide range of attractions that are accessible to customers with disabilities. Here's how to find the best experiences for you:

The official Disneyland Park website has a complete list of attractions organized by accessibility characteristics. You may filter attractions depending on your specific requirements (for example, accessible toilets or transfer seat availability).

Cast Member Assistance: Friendly Cast Members are always pleased to help you choose attractions that meet your specific needs. Don't be afraid to ask for help!

Remember that accessibility features and offers may differ based on the attraction. For further information, always visit the Disneyland Park website or ask a Cast Member.

## Dietary Accommodations

Disneyland Park accommodates a wide range of dietary requirements. This is what you should know.

**Special Dietary Requests:** Many restaurants include vegetarian, vegan, and gluten-free choices. When booking a dinner reservation, make sure to notify the restaurant of any dietary restrictions.

**Allergy Awareness:** Cast members at food establishments get comprehensive allergy training. Please do not hesitate to inquire about ingredients and allergies information.

**Guest Assistance Center:** Located near the Main Entrance, the Guest Assistance Center will help you identify eateries that meet your dietary requirements.

Pro Tip: Use a mobile meal ordering app, such as the Disneyland app, to peruse menus ahead of time and make special requests at participating places. This can save you time waiting in line and help you select appropriate meal alternatives.

## Assistance Animals

Disneyland Park allows well-behaved service animals that are trained to assist people with disabilities. Here are some recommendations to guarantee a smooth visit for you and your pet:

**Service Animal Identification:** Service animals must wear a harness or other visible identification that indicates their working duty.

**Leash or Harness:** Service animals must be leashed or harnessed at all times when visiting the park.

**Clean Up:** Guests are responsible for picking up after their service animals.

**Restricted locations:** Service animals are not permitted in some locations, such as kitchens and backstage areas.

Pro-Tip: Disneyland Park suggests bringing paperwork from a qualified healthcare practitioner confirming your service animal's training and purpose. Although not essential, this paperwork helps speed up the admission process.

## Special Passes and Privileges

Disneyland Park provides unique activities and benefits to people with impairments.

As previously stated, this complimentary service allows customers with disabilities who may struggle to wait in queues to register for a return time for specific attractions.

**Boarding Pass Accommodations:** Guests with disabilities may be eligible for modified boarding procedures at some attractions. For further information, speak with one of the cast members.

**Restroom Access Permit:** With this permit, guests with disabilities who require regular restroom access can use any restroom in the park, regardless of location.

Remember that to enjoy these exclusive services and perks, you may need to visit Guest Relations upon arrival at the park and produce the necessary credentials.

Guests with disabilities may enjoy a fantastic and inclusive experience at Disneyland Park by planning ahead of time, being acquainted with accessible resources, and making use of the supportive services provided by the park. The park's commitment to accessibility guarantees that everyone can experience the wonder, cultivating a sense of inclusion and belonging. Whether it's riding a thrilling roller coaster together, eating a great dinner with loved ones, or simply admiring the wonderful environment, Disneyland Park offers unique and unforgettable experiences for guests of all abilities. So come one, come all, and join us on a voyage of wonder and inclusion in the world's happiest spot!

# Chapter 12

# Safe and Sound: A Guide to Safety and Security at Disneyland Park

A visit to Disneyland Park should be full of fun, excitement, and lasting memories. However, prioritizing your safety and well-being is critical. This chapter will help you navigate the park with confidence and prepare for any circumstance.

## Park Rules & Regulations

Disneyland Park follows a set of rules and regulations to ensure the safety and enjoyment of all guests. Here are some important aspects to remember:

**Age Requirements:** Certain attractions have height or age requirements for safety reasons. Check these rules before lining up for a ride, especially if you're visiting with young children.

Smoking and tobacco use are strictly forbidden throughout the park, except designated outdoor smoking places.

Outside food and beverages are not permitted in the park, with only a few exceptions for medical or dietary reasons.

**Lines & Wait Times:** Queues can be long, particularly during peak seasons and at popular attractions. Respect the established queues and be patient with other visitors.

Disneyland has a strong "no line jumping" policy. Everyone waits their time, regardless of age or party size.

**Respectful Conduct:** Disruptive conduct, swearing, and violence will not be permitted. Disneyland tries to provide a friendly and inclusive atmosphere for all visitors.

Pro-Tip: Before you come, download the Disneyland Park app. The app lets you check wait times for attractions, find toilets, and peruse park laws and regulations for a fast refresher.

## Lost and Found

Misplacing a prized keepsake or beloved property might ruin your beautiful day. Here's what to do if you're in a lost item situation:

**Report Lost Items:** The initial step is to contact the local Guest Relations facility. Cast Members would gladly help you in completing a lost-and-found report.

**Lost and Found Locations:** Disneyland Park has two primary Lost and Found locations: one at Guest Relations at the Main Entrance, and another at Lost and Found near the Disneyland Railroad exit in Tomorrowland.

**Lost and Found Claiming:** If you locate a lost item, please give it into any Cast Mtor. They will guarantee that it is handed to the Lost & Found section.

Pro tip: Label your stuff with your name and contact information. This greatly enhances the likelihood of your lost item being returned to you.

## Emergency Services

In the event of an emergency, prompt medical assistance is required. This's what you should know.

**First Aid Centers:** Trained medical personnel run first aid stations around Disneyland Park. In the event of a minor accident or sickness, you can get help at these sites.

**Emergency Response:** Disneyland Park has a well-equipped emergency response crew ready to tackle any incident. If you encounter a significant medical emergency, please notify a Cast Member immediately.

**Fire Safety:** Extinguishers and emergency exits are strategically located around the park. Familiarize yourself with the emergency exits around you, especially if you're approaching a new region of the park.

Remember: In any emergency, prioritize your own and others' safety. Notify a Cast Member or a park security officer immediately.

## Health and Safety Guidelines

A healthier, happier you means a more spectacular Disneyland trip! Here are some health and safety guidelines to bear in mind:

**Hydration:** Staying hydrated is especially important on hot summer days. Carry a refillable water bottle and drink often throughout the day. Water fountains and hydration stations are spread around the park.

**Sun Protection:** The California sun may be intense. Use sunscreen generously and reapply every two hours, especially after swimming or sweating. Consider wearing a hat and sunglasses to provide extra protection.

**Comfortable Footwear:** Disneyland Park requires a lot of walking. Wear comfortable shoes with adequate support.

Be prepared for the weather conditions. Check the forecast before you go and pack appropriately.

**Pre-existing medical issues:** If you have any pre-existing medical issues, make sure you bring any essential medications with you and notify a traveling partner in case of an emergency.

Pro tip: Download the Disneyland Park app and use the useful wait time function. This helps you to carefully arrange your day and avoid spending too much time waiting in long lines under the blazing sun.

By following these suggestions and being acquainted with the park's safety precautions, you can ensure a worry-free and pleasurable visit to Disneyland Park.

## Chapter 13

## Beyond the Magic Gates: Exploring Paris and the Environs

B onjour! Disneyland Park provides an amazing world behind its walls, but stepping outside its confines reveals a richness of cultural experiences and hidden jewels. This chapter will lead you through interesting day trip possibilities that complement your Disneyland Park journey, converting your Paris holiday into a tapestry of thrilling amusement parks, historical sights, and luxurious leisure.

## Jurassic Park at Disneyland

Jurassic Park at Disneyland, though not an official part of Disneyland itself, is a thrilling attraction featured prominently at Universal Studios theme parks. This immersive experience draws visitors into the world of the iconic movie series, where dinosaurs roam once again through cutting-edge animatronics and lifelike environments.

In Jurassic Park: The Ride at Universal Studios Hollywood (34.1371° N, 118.3553° W), guests embark on a river adventure that starts serenely, showcasing gentle giants like Brachiosaurus. Suddenly, the tour takes a dramatic turn as guests navigate through areas overrun by predatory dinosaurs, culminating in a heart-stopping 85-foot drop.

At Universal's Islands of Adventure in Orlando (28.4744° N, 81.4677° W), the VelociCoaster offers an intense roller coaster experience. Riders are launched through the Velociraptor paddock at speeds up to 70 mph, facing inversions and near-miss elements that make this one of the most exhilarating rides.

For those seeking educational engagement, the Jurassic Park Discovery Center provides interactive exhibits and live demonstrations on dinosaur genetics and paleontology. Additionally, the Raptor Encounter offers a close-up meeting with a life-like Velociraptor, perfect for photo opportunities and learning.

Jurassic Park attractions blend excitement, education, and the magic of cinema, offering visitors a dynamic and unforgettable adventure.

## Paris City Highlights: A City Rich in History and Beauty

A journey to France isn't complete without experiencing the romance of Paris, the City of Light. Paris, steeped in history, romance, and artistic genius, provides a tantalizing combination of renowned sites, world-class museums, and lovely districts waiting to be discovered. Here are some must-see places to include on your Paris itinerary:

The Eiffel Tower (Champ de Mars, 5 Av. Gustave Eiffel, 75007 Paris, France) is unquestionably Paris' most iconic landmark, a wrought-iron masterpiece that pierces the city's skyline. Ascend to the peak (by stairs or elevator) for spectacular panoramic views of the city spread out before you. Admire the complex latticework design and take great images from this renowned vantage point.

**Eiffel Tower, Paris**
Louvre Museum (Rue de Rivoli, 75001 Paris, France): Immerse yourself in the world's best art collection, located in the majestic Louvre Museum. This museum, housed in the Louvre Palace, a former royal palace, features an extraordinary collection that spans ages and cultures. Walk through large galleries and admire treasures such as Leonardo da Vinci's Mona Lisa, Venus de Milo, and numerous more works that have influenced human history and artistic expression.

**Louvre Museum, Paris**
www.louvre.fr
Musée d'Orsay (1 Rue de la Légion d'Honneur, 75007 Paris, France): Add to your creative adventure by visiting the Musée d'Orsay, which is located across the Seine River from the Louvre. This museum has an amazing collection of Impressionist and Post-Impressionist art, including works by famous painters like Monet, Renoir, Van Gogh, and Cézanne.

The museum itself is a stunning Beaux-Arts structure that adds to the whole visual experience.

**Musée d'Orsay, Paris**
Notre Dame Cathedral (6 Parvis Notre-Dame - Pl. Jean-Paul II, 75004 Paris, France): Admire the architectural magnificence of Notre Dame Cathedral, a UNESCO World Heritage Site and Paris' spiritual heart for centuries. Admire the magnificent flying buttresses, stained-glass windows portraying biblical events, and the distinctive gargoyles atop the cathedral. While a tragic fire in 2019 severely destroyed the cathedral, restoration activities are continuing, and visitors may still appreciate the exterior and learn about its rich history.

**Notre-Dame Cathedral, Paris**
Arc de Triomphe (Place Charles de Gaulle, 75008 Paris, France): Celebrate French victory at the Arc de Triomphe, a magnificent arch at the western end of the Champs-Élysées boulevard. Napoleon Bonaparte commissioned the arch in 1806, to celebrate triumphs in the French Revolution and Napoleonic Wars. Climb to the summit for panoramic views of the Champs-Élysées and learn about the historic significance of this Parisian monument.

### Arc de Triomphe, Paris

Insider Tip: Consider obtaining a Paris Pass, a multi-day pass that includes admission to numerous major attractions such as the Louvre Museum and the Eiffel Tower, as well as public transit use. This can be a cost-effective method to see the city's main attractions without having to buy separate tickets for each.

These are only a few of Paris' numerous intriguing landmarks. Beyond these, visit attractive areas such as Montmartre, which has cobblestone streets and the Sacré-Coeur church, or the old Latin Quarter, which is noted for its academic ambiance and bustling cafés.

## Château de Versailles: A glimpse into French opulence

Step back in time and see the majesty of the Palace of Versailles, a UNESCO World Heritage Site just outside of Paris (Place de la Château, 78000 Versailles, France). This opulent palace was the primary residence of the French kings from the 17th to the 18th century and is now a symbol of French monarchy and power.

**Château de Versailles**

Wander through the State Apartments and see the epitome of French royal grandeur, including the sumptuous Hall of Mirrors, a large gallery lined with floor-to-ceiling mirrors that produces a stunning display. Explore the King's and Queen's Grand Apartments, private chambers designated for the monarchs and furnished with fine furnishings, tapestries, and paintings that provide an insight into the royal lifestyle. Pay close attention to the numerous features throughout the palace, from the gilded moldings to the painted ceilings, as each aspect demonstrates the creative brilliance of the time.

Wander through carefully designed grounds: Step beyond the palace to discover Versailles' extensive gardens. These gardens, designed by famous landscape architect André Le Nôtre, are masterpieces of French formal gardening. Stroll through the groomed hedges, marvel at the carefully sculpted topiaries, and observe the several fountains that come to life throughout the day with music-synchronized water performances.

Explore the magnificent carriages on display at the Gallery of Coaches. This collection includes several horse-drawn carriages used by the royal family for ceremonial events and daily journeys. Admire the workmanship and beauty on display in the carriages, each of which reflects the grandeur of the French court.

Pro Tip: Allow plenty of time for your visit to Versailles, since the palace and gardens are huge and fascinating. Consider purchasing your tickets online in advance to avoid long lines, particularly during high season. Audio tours are available for rent and provide informative commentary on the palace's history and significance.

Versailles provides a fascinating peek into the luxury and grandeur of the French monarchy. Soak up the sumptuous ambiance, stroll around the perfectly manicured gardens, and picture yourself transported to a bygone period of absolute power and creative magnificence.

## Parc Astérix

Calling all thrill enthusiasts! Parc Astérix, located just north of Paris (Rue du Bois des Moutiers, 60128 Plailly, France), provides an exciting alternative to Paris' historical and cultural attractions. This Gaul-themed amusement park is inspired by the iconic French comic book series "Asterix" and offers a day full of thrilling rides, family-friendly attractions, and engaging performances.

## Parc Astérix

Experience the adrenaline rush of exciting coasters: Parc Astérix has a large range of roller coasters catering to varying excitement levels. Test your daring on Goudurix, a spinning coaster that takes riders on a whirlwind experience, or scream with glee on Tonnerre de Zeus, a wooden racing coaster that can reach speeds of up to 60 mph.

Take a break from the adrenaline thrill and enjoy the live entertainment options available throughout the park. Attend a live-action performance starring Asterix and his companions, meet the characters, or be captivated by spectacular daredevil displays.

Explore La Gaule town, a reproduction of a Gaulish village from the comics, and immerse yourself in the universe of Asterix. Wander through thatched-roof cottages, see traditional artisan displays, and try Gaulish food.

Pro-Tip: If you want to visit both Disneyland Park and Parc Astérix, consider purchasing a multi-day ticket that includes admission to both parks. This might be a cost-effective choice, particularly if you want to spend many days at each site. Check the park's website for any special events or seasonal activities that may be taking place while you visit.

Parc Astérix provides a fun-filled vacation for both families and thrill-seekers. Experience the world of Asterix come to life, overcome your anxieties on thrilling rides, and have unforgettable moments with your loved ones.

## Vald'Europe Shopping Center: A Shopaholic's Paradise

After your exciting theme park activities, treat yourself to some retail therapy at Val d'Europe, a massive shopping complex located just outside of Disneyland Park (Rue du Québec, 77700 Serris, France). This shopper's paradise has a wide variety of retailers, restaurants, and entertainment options, making it an excellent place to spend a relaxing afternoon.

val-d-europe-en.klepierre.fr

**Val d'Europe Shopping Centre**

Browse a varied choice of stores: from well-known luxury labels like Gucci and Prada to high-street favorites like H&M and Zara, Val d'Europe caters to all budgets and tastes. Discover a wide range of boutiques providing apparel, accessories, gadgets, souvenirs, and much more. Whether you're looking for a unique Parisian gift or just want to update your wardrobe, you'll find something to fit your preferences.

**Enjoy wonderful cuisine:** After a day of shopping, visit one of Val d'Europe's many restaurants and cafés. You may enjoy a wide range of cuisines here, from traditional French meals to cosmopolitan favorites like Italian pasta and Japanese sushi. Enjoy a fast bite at a café, a leisurely dinner at a sit-down restaurant, or a sweet treat from a bakery.

**Catch the newest movie releases:** The multiplex theater in Val d'Europe shows the latest blockbusters and indie films. This sophisticated theater complex has comfortable seats, cutting-edge equipment, and a range of concession options, making it the ideal spot to relax after a day of shopping or touring.

Pro tip: Val d'Europe provides a quick tax refund service for overseas guests. Purchases bought at stores with the tax-free shopping emblem qualify for a VAT (Value Added Tax) rebate. Before making any purchases, make sure to learn about the procedure and eligibility conditions.

Val d'Europe is a shoppers' paradise. This retail center has everything for everyone, from high-end clothes to scrumptious cuisine and cutting-edge entertainment alternatives. So gather your shopping bags and prepare for a retail therapy session!

Aquatonic spa: rejuvenation after a day of adventure.
Aquatonic Paris Val d'Europe (5 Rue du Lac, 77700 Serris, France) will help you relax and soothe your sore muscles after a day of seeing Parisian attractions and amusement parks. This luxury spa provides a haven of relaxation and regeneration, ideal for recharging before your next trip.
www.groupon.fr

## Aquatonic Spa

Unwind in a range of pools: Immerse yourself in pools with varying water temperatures and therapeutic advantages. Float in the weightless experience of the Dead Sea pool, relax in the warm hydrotherapy pools, or increase circulation in the stimulating cold water pool. Each pool provides a distinct experience that promotes relaxation and well-being.

Treat yourself to a revitalizing massage or body treatment that is tailored to your unique requirements. The spa program includes a wide range of services, including deep tissue massages and aromatherapy. Allow the professional therapists to relieve your tension and leave you feeling rejuvenated and energized.

Escape the hustle and bustle of city life and immerse yourself in the quiet atmosphere of the Aquatonic Spa. Dimmed lights, calming music, and cozy relaxation spaces provide a peaceful and serene environment.

Pro-Tip: Book your spa treatments ahead of time, especially during weekends and busy seasons, to ensure your preferred time slot. The spa also provides customized packages that combine pool admission with massages or other treatments, allowing you to build your own spa experience.

Aquatonic Spa is a must-see for those looking for a luxurious and soothing experience. Soothe your body and mind, and you'll emerge feeling renewed and eager to see more of what Paris and its surroundings have to offer.

By stepping outside the gates of Disneyland Park and experiencing the numerous possibilities available in this region, you can make your Parisian holiday an unforgettable one.

# Chapter 14

# Frequently Asked Questions - Navigating Your Parisian Adventure Easily

A vacation to Paris promises to be a memorable voyage packed with breathtaking views, wonderful cuisine, and engaging encounters. However, navigating a new city might be difficult. This chapter answers some commonly asked questions (FAQs) to give you the information and confidence to fully enjoy your Parisian journey.

## Common Inquiries

**Which is the ideal time to visit Paris?**
The response is based on your selections. Spring (April-May) and autumn (September-October) provide lovely weather and manageable crowds. Summer (June to August) has more daylight hours but can be congested and hot. Winter (November-March) has the lowest prices and fewer visitors, while certain attractions may have reduced hours.

**How can I get about Paris?**
Paris has an efficient public transit network, which includes the metro (subway), buses, and RER trains. Purchasing a Paris Visite travel card allows you unrestricted travel within defined zones for a set period. Taxis and ride-sharing applications are also available, although negotiating traffic may be time-consuming.

**Which currency is used in Paris?**
The Euro (€) is the official currency of France. ATMs and currency exchange agencies are easily accessible around the city. Consider telling your bank about your vacation intentions to avoid any problems while using your cards overseas.

**Do I have to speak French?**
While basic French words are always welcomed, English is commonly spoken in tourist regions. Learning a few key French words, such as "Bonjour" (hello), "Merci" (thank you), and "S'il vous plait" (please), will greatly improve your relationships with locals.

**What should I bring for my trip?**
Pack comfortable walking shoes because you'll probably be doing a lot of exploration. The weather might be unpredictable, so dress in layers. An umbrella and a reusable water bottle are always useful. Make sure to check the weather prediction before your trip to ensure you prepare appropriately.

**What are some essentials to bring?**
A comfortable backpack, a universal adapter for your electronic gadgets, a phrasebook or translation program, and a duplicate of your passport and other documents are all advised. Consider buying travel insurance for peace of mind.

## Tips from Experienced Visitors

Get tickets in advance: To avoid long lines at popular attractions, get tickets online ahead of time. Many attractions have timed entrance slots, which allow you to avoid the regular admission wait.

**Enjoy the walking culture:** Paris is a pedestrian-friendly city. Walking helps you to uncover hidden gems and absorb the local culture. Comfortable walking shoes are necessary!

**Sample the local food:** To sample true French cuisine, go beyond cafes and into local eateries. Don't be hesitant to try different foods; you could find your new favorite!

**Learn a few fundamental French phrases:** Knowing a few key French phrases can help you engage more effectively with locals. Even a simple "bonjour" (hello) demonstrates respect for the culture.

**Pack lightweight and adaptable clothing:** Layering helps you to adjust to changing weather. Choose neutral hues and mix-and-match items to create numerous ensembles for your vacation.

**Respect local customs and clothing rules:** When visiting religious sites, dress modestly. Be careful of noise levels in public places, and avoid eating when on public transit.

## Troubleshooting and Problem-solving

If you find yourself lost in the city, don't panic! Look for a metro station or a familiar sight. Most Parisians are glad to assist if you ask for directions nicely. Having downloaded map or offline navigation software on your phone might be helpful.

**Language barrier?** Use a phrasebook, a translation tool, or point to illustrations on menus. Many Parisians understand rudimentary English, and gestures may frequently communicate your demands.

**Transportation Issues:** If you face a metro closure or a bus delay, look for alternate routes or use ride-sharing applications. Having a rudimentary awareness of the public transit system might help you avoid unforeseen circumstances.

**Minor theft:** Be mindful of your surroundings, especially in busy situations. Keep valuables safe, and avoid carrying significant amounts of cash. Report any theft to the local authorities right once.

If you are feeling poorly, many pharmacies in Paris sell basic drugs. For more significant medical issues, find the local hospital or clinic. Consider obtaining travel insurance with medical coverage for peace of mind.

By familiarizing yourself with these frequently asked questions and advice, you'll be more prepared to face any obstacles that may emerge throughout your Paris vacation. Remember that part of the travel experience is accepting the unexpected and learning to adjust. Relax, have fun, and embrace the spirit of exploration!

# Chapter 15

# Final Tips and Advice for Polishing Your Parisian Gem

As your Parisian vacation approaches, here are some final pieces of advice to guarantee a seamless and memorable experience:

## Making the Most of Your Visit: Enjoy the Parisian Pace

Accept the art of leisurely living: Parisians value relishing life's simple pleasures. Linger over leisurely lunches, take lengthy walks down the Seine, and avoid the temptation to rush from one thing to the next. Immerse yourself in the city's laid-back vibe and admire the beauty that surrounds you.

**Venture beyond the tourist trail:** While prominent landmarks are worth visiting, don't be afraid to explore lovely districts like Montmartre or Le Marais. Wander down picturesque streets, discover secret cafés, and drink up the true Parisian atmosphere.

**Engage with the locals:** A pleasant "Bonjour" (good day) goes a long way. Engage in talks with merchants, waiters, or other passengers. Learning a few simple French words shows respect for the culture and can lead to wonderful experiences.

**Embrace serendipity:** Plan your agenda with allowance for improvisation. Take a detour down an interesting side street, visit an unexpected museum, or simply relax in a park and people-watch. Unexpected discoveries can lead to some of life's most unforgettable events.

Remember that your Parisian vacation will be tailored to your interests and preferences. Don't feel obligated to stick to a set agenda; instead, be open to new experiences and make memories that will last a lifetime.

## Insider Tips: Paris Secrets Revealed

**Picnic in the park:** Buy baguettes, cheese, cured meats, and fresh fruit from a local market and have a delicious picnic lunch in a Parisian park like Jardin du Luxembourg or Champ de Mars. Soak in the sunshine, people-watch, and enjoy the simple pleasures.

**Free museum days:** Many Parisian museums provide free admission on specified days or evenings. Research these chances in advance to get a cultural experience without breaking the wallet.

Rent a bicycle and discover Paris on two wheels. Cycling allows you to travel further than walking, explore lovely backstreets, and see the city from a fresh viewpoint.

Take a Seine River boat and see classic monuments like the Eiffel Tower and Notre Dame from a fresh perspective. Choose between a midday sightseeing cruise and a romantic nighttime option that includes supper.

Learn about French wine: Participate in a wine-tasting event to learn the many flavors of French wines. Many wine bars and shops provide guided tastings, where you may learn about different varieties and combinations.

Remember, these are just a few insider ideas to help you get started. With a little investigation and adventure, you're bound to find your own hidden jewels and Parisian secrets.

## Packing List: Essentials for a Paris Adventure

**Comfortable walking shoes:** Paris is a pedestrian-friendly city, so comfortable walking shoes are essential. To manage cobblestone streets and long treks, use shoes that provide adequate support.

**Versatile clothing:** Bring a variety of layers to accommodate changing weather. Neutral hues and mix-and-match pieces will allow you to create a variety of ensembles during your journey. Remember to pack a scarf, hat, and sunglasses for enhanced comfort. French power outlets have two circular prongs, thus a travel adapter is required to charge your electrical gadgets.

Staying hydrated is crucial, and using a reusable water bottle allows you to be more environmentally conscious while enjoying the city. Save money by refilling your bottle at public fountains or cafés.

**Small backpack:** A comfy backpack is great for transporting things such as your camera, guidebook, water bottle, and mementos on your vacation.

Remember to pack light! You'll probably be doing a lot of walking, and navigating the subway with heavy bags might be difficult. If you'll be there for a lengthy amount of time, consider doing your laundry while there.

## Departure Day Tips: Ensure a Smooth Takeoff

Double-check your passport and travel papers. Make sure your passport is valid for at least six months after your trip dates, and that you have all applicable visas or permissions. Make copies of your passport and other critical documents to ensure their safety in the event of loss.

Confirm your flight and transportation arrangements. Check your flight timings, gate numbers, and any pre-booked transportation options, such as airport shuttles or taxis.

**Pack necessities in your carry-on bag:** Keep a change of clothing, prescriptions, and any valuables in your carry-on luggage in case checked baggage is delayed. Download any ebooks, audiobooks, or movies you intend to watch on the journey to your carry-on for amusement. Pack any basic toiletries you could need for the trip.

**Allow plenty of time for airport security:** Arrive at the airport long before your trip to minimize last-minute stress. Familiarize yourself with airport security processes and provide additional time for any lines.

**Embrace the journey:** Departure day might be frantic, but take a deep breath and think about the amazing experience that awaits you in Paris. Spend your trip relaxing, reading a book, or listening to music.

Remember that with a little planning and preparation, your departure day may be easy and stress-free. So, complete your plans, fill your luggage with Parisian fantasies, and prepare to embark on an incredible vacation!

# Conclusion

Ah, the flickering gaslights, the perfume of freshly cooked croissants, and the iconic silhouette of the Eiffel Tower piercing the Paris skyline. Your Disney Paris trip awaits, a world intertwined with timeless charm and exhilarating magic. This handbook has been your faithful companion, methodically laying out a course through laughter, amazement, and memories sweeter than spun sugar.

But remember, darling visitor, that the magic stretches well beyond the gates of Disneyland Park. Paris is a symphony of history, culture, and delicious treats ready to be savored. This city, a living museum, tells stories from bygone ages via its great architecture and renowned sites. Climb the Eiffel Tower and feel the world beneath your feet, or explore the Louvre's labyrinthine hallways, where artworks whisper secrets from centuries past.

At a lovely sidewalk café, sip espresso and take up the Parisian atmosphere to experience the city's essence. For the daring gourmet, a world of culinary creation awaits. From Michelin-starred restaurants to modest local bistros, Parisian food is a symphony of tastes eager to entice your palate. Beyond the classic attractions, discover hidden gems such as a beautiful bookstore nestled away on a cobblestone street, a busy market brimming with fresh food, and a tranquil park ideal for a picnic under the Parisian sky.

This manual has taught you how to traverse the parks, overcome thrilling rides, and meet your favorite Disney characters. However, the ultimate enchantment is found in accepting the unexpected. Take a detour down a side street that piques your interest, start up a discussion with a local over a hot cup of coffee, or simply enjoy the simple pleasure of people watching in the park. Embrace the Parisian ethos of "joie de vivre," or pleasure of life, and allow the city to enchant you.

So, dear tourist, when you go, carry a little of Parisian enchantment with you. Allow Mickey Mouse's lingering laughter to blend with the whispers of history that resonate through the city streets. Your Parisian excursion was more than simply a trip; it was a tapestry woven with exciting experiences, cultural discoveries, and memories that will always have a hint of fairy dust.

# Appendix

Resources and Contacts: A Parisian Lifeline

A successful Parisian vacation involves not just meticulous preparation, but also access to dependable resources and relationships. This section provides a comprehensive list of vital phone numbers, official websites, and applications, as well as useful travel agents and tour operators.

**Important Phone Numbers:**

Emergency Services: 112 (This is the single emergency number for police, ambulance, and fire services in France.)

Police: 17

Medical Emergency: 15 (Connects you to the SAMU service, France's national emergency medical service).

Fire Department: 18

Lost and Found: 08 21 00 25 (Lost and Found Office in Paris)

Taxi Services: Several taxi firms operate in Paris. You can hail a cab on the street or contact one of the following companies:

Contact Alpha Taxi at +33 (0)1 47 33 22 22 or G7 Taxi at +33 (0)1 47 33 70 00.

Remember to have these important phone numbers on your phone or jot them down in a notepad for quick access in case of need.

**Official Websites and Apps**
Paris Tourist Office: https://www.parisjetaime.com/eng (Offers detailed information on attractions, transportation, events, and more.)
RATP (the Paris Public Transportation Network): https://www.ratp.fr/ (Provides real-time timetables for metro, bus, RER, and trams, as well as route maps and ticket alternatives)
Navigo Easy (Public Transit Pass): https://www.iledefrance-mobilites.fr/titres-et-tarifs/supports/passe-navigo-easy (Official website for ordering and administering the Navigo Easy travel card for unlimited travel within specified zones.)
Louvre Museum website: https://www.louvre.fr/. (Provides information on exhibitions, tickets, opening hours, and tourist tips.)
The Palace of Versailles: https://en.chateauversailles.fr/discover/estate/palace (Offers information on visiting the palace, gardens, and estate, including ticket choices and guided tours.)

Pro-Tip: Before your trip, download these official apps and familiarize yourself with the websites to improve your navigation and overall Paris experience.

**Travel agents and tour operators**
Viator website: https://www.viator.com (Provides a wide selection of excursions and activities in Paris, from skip-the-line tickets for major sights to day trips to other regions).
GetYourGuide: https://www.getyourguide.com/c/step-by-step-in-listing-your-activity-on-getyourguide. (Offers a variety of excursions and experiences in Paris, including culinary tours, bike tours, and walking tours led by local guides.)
Context Travel (https://www.contexttravel.com) (Offers small-group, culturally intensive excursions conducted by skilled guides.)
Rick Steves Tours: https://www.ricksteves.com/tours. (Provides guided tours in Paris and other European sites, noted for their emphasis on cultural activities)
Local Parisian Travel businesses: Many Parisian travel businesses provide tailored excursions and experiences. Researching reliable agencies in Paris might yield distinct and authentic results.

Remember to consider your hobbies, travel style, and budget when selecting a travel agency or tour operator. Online reviews and pricing comparisons can help you locate the ideal match for your Paris excursion.

Using these resources and contacts, you'll be well-prepared to explore Paris with confidence and ease. So bookmark these sites, download the necessary applications, and keep a list of vital phone numbers available. With this knowledge at your fingertips, you're ready to go on an exciting Parisian experience!

## Glossary for Disney Paris Travel Guide 2024

1. **Adventureland**: A themed land featuring attractions based on adventure and exploration.
2. **Annual Pass**: A pass that offers unlimited access to the parks for a year, along with various discounts and benefits.
3. **Attraction**: A ride, show, or experience designed to entertain park guests.
4. **Autograph Book**: A book used to collect signatures from Disney characters.
5. **Character Meet and Greet**: An opportunity for guests to meet and take photos with Disney characters.
6. **Disney Village**: An entertainment complex featuring dining, shopping, and entertainment options.
7. **Extra Magic Time**: Exclusive early park access available to guests staying at Disney hotels.
8. **FastPass**: A system that allows guests to reserve access to popular attractions, reducing wait times.
9. **Fantasyland**: A themed land featuring attractions based on Disney's classic animated films.

Copytighted Material

10. **Frontierland**: A themed land inspired by the American Old West.
11. **Hotel New York - The Art of Marvel**: A Disney hotel themed around Marvel superheroes and New York City.
12. **Imagineers**: The creative team responsible for designing Disney parks, attractions, and resorts.
13. **Main Street, U.S.A.**: The entrance area of Disneyland Paris, designed to resemble a turn-of-the-century American town.
14. **Magic Kingdom**: The central theme park of Disneyland Paris, featuring various themed lands.
15. **Parade**: A procession of Disney characters and performers that takes place at scheduled times.
16. **Park Hopper Ticket**: A ticket that allows access to multiple parks on the same day.
17. **Photopass**: A service that provides professional photos taken around the parks, available for purchase or download.
18. **Pin Trading**: A popular activity where guests trade collectible pins with other guests and cast members.
19. **Pirates of the Caribbean**: A popular attraction featuring a boat ride through scenes of pirate adventures.

20. **Sleeping Beauty Castle**: The iconic centerpiece of Disneyland Paris, based on the fairy tale castle from "Sleeping Beauty."
21. **Souvenir**: A keepsake or memento purchased to remember the visit to Disneyland Paris.
22. **Star Wars Hyperspace Mountain**: A roller coaster attraction themed around the Star Wars universe.
23. **Ticket Booth**: A location where guests can purchase park admission tickets.
24. **Walt Disney Studios Park**: A theme park adjacent to Disneyland Park, featuring attractions based on movies and filmmaking.
25. **Wave Machine**: A feature in water attractions that creates artificial waves for an immersive experience.
26. **Annual Passholder**: A guest who holds an annual pass and enjoys exclusive benefits and discounts.
27. **Audio-Animatronics**: Robotic figures used in attractions to create lifelike movements and sounds.
28. **Backlot**: An area in Walt Disney Studios Park showcasing behind-the-scenes movie magic.

29. **Boutique**: A themed store selling Disney merchandise, apparel, and souvenirs.
30. **Cast Member**: A term for all Disney employees, from ride operators to performers.
31. **Concierge Service**: Personalized guest services provided at Disney hotels for dining reservations, tickets, and more.
32. **Dapper Dan's Haircuts**: A barbershop on Main Street, U.S.A., offering classic haircuts and shaves.
33. **Dark Ride**: An indoor ride that takes guests through a series of themed scenes, often with special effects and animatronics.
34. **Disney Dreams!**: A nighttime spectacular featuring fireworks, projections, and music over Sleeping Beauty Castle.
35. **Disneyland Railroad**: A train ride that circles Disneyland Park, offering scenic views and convenient transportation.
36. **E-ticket Attraction**: A term originating from Disneyland's ticket book system, referring to the most popular and exciting rides.
37. **Enchanted Passage**: A walkthrough attraction featuring dioramas of scenes from Disney fairy tales.

38. **Fantasyland Theatre**: A venue for live shows and performances featuring Disney characters.
39. **Festival of Pirates and Princesses**: A seasonal event with themed parades, shows, and character meet-and-greets.
40. **FastPass+**: An upgraded FastPass system allowing guests to reserve access to attractions before their visit.**Hopper Ticket**: A ticket allowing guests to visit both Disneyland Park and Walt Disney Studios Park on the same day.
41. **Imagineering**: The combination of "imagination" and "engineering," referring to the creative process of designing Disney attractions.
42. **Liberty Arcade**: A covered walkway on Main Street, U.S.A., showcasing exhibits about the Statue of Liberty and American history.
43. **Mickey's PhilharMagic**: A 3D show featuring scenes and songs from popular Disney animated films.
44. **Parc Disneyland**: The French name for Disneyland Park, the main theme park at Disneyland Paris.
45. **PhotoPass+**: An enhanced PhotoPass service offering unlimited digital downloads of professional photos taken around the parks.

46. **Quick Service Restaurant**: Dining locations offering fast, casual meals without table service.
47. **Ratatouille: The Adventure**: A 4D dark ride based on the Disney-Pixar film "Ratatouille."
48. **RunDisney**: A series of themed running events and races held at Disneyland Paris.

Printed in Great Britain
by Amazon